# FRONT ROW

## Evenings at the Theatre

### Pieces from *The Oldie*

## BERYL BAINBRIDGE

continuum
LONDON • NEW YORK

**Continuum**

The Tower Building, 11 York Road, London SE1 7NX
15 East 26th Street, New York NY 10010

www.continuumbooks.com

First published 2005

**British Library Cataloguing-in-Publication Data**
A catalogue record for this book is available from the British Library.

ISBN: 0–8264–8787–4

The reviews in this volume were first published in *The Oldie*.
John Betjeman's poem *Sun and Fun* copyright © John Betjeman estate.
Philip Larkin's poem *Annus Mirabilis* used with permission of
Faber & Faber.
Stills taken from *Coronation Street* © used with permission of
Granada Television.

Typeset by Kenneth Burnley, Wirral, Cheshire
Printed and bound in Great Britain by MPG Books Ltd,
Bodmin, Cornwall

# Contents

# CONTENTS

# CONTENTS

# CONTENTS

# Introduction

At a luncheon in 1991 Richard Ingrams announced his intention of launching a magazine to be called *The Oldie*. The title did not necessarily mean that the publication would target readers reliant on bath-chairs and zimmer frames, merely give an indication that it might interest persons more concerned with the avoidance of death duties than the collecting of pop records or an ascent of Mount Everest. It would contain political comments of a satirical kind, reminiscences of the past, advice on keeping one's money safe, places of interest to visit, book, theatre and music reviews and a column listing the best wines to buy. The second edition of *The Oldie* did indeed contain an article by Dr Tom asserting that drink was a medical necessity for those over fifty, though to be fair he did say in moderation. Fired by Richard's enthusiasm, I immediately volunteered to write the theatre reviews.

For those wondering what qualifications it requires to take on such an intellectual task, it should be borne in mind that I was not a stranger to the world of the stage. At the age of five I became a member of the Thelma Bickerstaff tap-dancing troupe appearing at the Garrick Theatre, Southport. Four years later I went solo and sang *Kiss Me Goodnight Sergeant Major* to an audience of wounded soldiers transported from the local hospital.

In those far-off days it was considered important for people to talk properly; even a job as a shop assistant required a knowledge of the correct pronunciation of standard English. Consequently, I was later sent to elocution lessons at the Crane Hall in Liverpool, where I intoned

'How now, brown cow' and 'Claire has fair hair' under the strict supervision of Mrs Ackerley, an imposing lady notable for her orange hair and gold cigarette holder.

I was eleven or twelve years old when my mother read in the *Liverpool Echo* that child actors were needed for Northern Children's Hour. Taken on, I spent the next two years, along with Billie Whitelaw, Sandra and Judith Chalmers, Brian Trueman and Tony Warren – that little lad with the big ears who thought up *Coronation Street* – performing in various dramas. The only one I remember was a sort of documentary to do with careers, in which I was employed as a stable-hand and talked of the importance of withers. I also juggled coconuts to mimic the sound of galloping hooves while shouting 'Hey up, Neddy.'

We were under the instruction of Uncle Herbert, Uncle Trevor and Auntie Nan MacDonald. Griselda Hervey, who married a Lord, Henry Ainlee, the silent screen actor, and Fred Fairclough – not to be confused with Len in *Coronation Street* – played our Mums and Dads. Fred wore a red cravat and cavalry twill trousers. Griselda rehearsed in a hat with a feather and wore a silver fox cape slung round her shoulders. If Fred fluffed his lines he'd work his false teeth up and down in a passion and shout 'Gawd Almighty' at which Auntie Nan, glaring at him, would tap her pencil on her script until he murmured, 'Sorry infants, slip of the impure tongue.'

It was after this experience that I was expelled from school and exiled to Tring in Hertfordshire to continue my dramatic training; we were housed in a mansion built by Charles II for Nell Gwynn. Unfortunately, it turned out to be a ballet school, and I was no good at that sort of dancing.

My time there, however, was not entirely wasted, for one holiday I was invited home by a dormitory chum who lived in Derbyshire. On arrival at the station in Bullwell we spied a poster advertising a talent contest at the Variety Theatre. Entering, we won, the prize being a week's engagement. Our opening number was based on a song made popular by Billy Cotton, 'Hang on the Bell, Nellie'. We swung on to the stage on ropes. Next came a joint rendering of 'Abdul the Bulbul Emir', followed by the umbrella routine from *Singing in the Rain.*

On the bill we came between the comedian Dave King, and Monty and his Talking Wonder Dogs. Twice nightly I teetered on a wooden crate, heart thudding, hands gripping the rope, my ankle held by the prop man lest I should spill forward before my time and form a double act with Mr King. When the comedian bounded into the wings and the lights dimmed and the circus roll of drums began in the orchestra pit, I swung out over the stage, spotlight swooping in pursuit, flashing across the backcloth like Tinkerbell in Never Never Land, and descended with a thud into the very centre of an illusion. It was not that I found the applause gratifying or the experience ever less than terrifying, but there was a moment when fear and embarrassment lifted and I was no longer trapped within myself. For one moment I floated free and aimless as the specks of dust shimmering like fireflies above the footlights.

A year later I was employed as an assistant stage manager – unpaid – at the Playhouse Theatre, Liverpool. Aged sixteen and lacking any academic qualifications, I was provided with an unique form of higher education. I had to choose props for the set; read up on the plays of Ibsen, Shakespeare and Ben Travers; work out the change from purchases of sausage rolls; sit in the prompt corner with the script; help out in the wardrobe department; make sure the coal-bucket in the green room was always full; coax Mr X from the betting shop and be ready at all times to procure ice-packs and aspirins for Miss Y.

It was a repertory company of four actresses and eight actors: of the latter all but one had served in the war. The other seven, including the producer, presumably as a result of the experience had become converted to the Catholic faith. The priests from the local church, who were not allowed to go to a theatre once the doors opened to the public, came to the dress rehearsals and blessed the productions. I wore a large wooden cross tucked into my ankle sock.

Apart from walking on in *Richard II* and playing a dog in *The Tinder Box*, no important roles came my way until a youth from Scotland was unable to appear in a play about a boy mathematical genius and I was promptly marched off to the barbers to have my hair cut. I next played Ptolomy in Shaw's *Caesar and Cleopatra*, and a hostile witness in a courtroom drama called *Madame Conti*.

My new profession under way I decamped for London, arriving as Mr Atlee was about to depart and Mr Churchill to return. While awaiting my summons to Hollywood I got a job as an usherette in a cinema in the Tottenham Court Road. I saw *Cyrano de Bergerac* 37 times. When I lost this employment – something nasty in the woodshed to do with the cinema manager – I bounced by trolly-car every Friday morning from Hampstead to Islington to collect my fifteen shillings dole money. Afterwards, in a cafe near Collins' Music Hall, I ate my only breakfast of the week: fried bread, egg, sausage and tomato. On the wall opposite hung a poster of Tilly the Tassel Queen, bosoms now swirled to dust, she who had twice nightly tied ribbons to her nipples and spun them round and round.

A year later I appeared in *Hobson's Choice* at the Arts Theatre alongside Jill Bennett and Donald Pleasance. There followed repertory seasons in Windsor, Salisbury, Warrington and Dundee. Salisbury was memorable for the attentions of a Lieutenant Gopsil, victim of the First World War and now incarcerated in the local mental institution. He wrote to my father asking him to foot the bill for our forthcoming marriage. Dundee was equally interesting; an actor chained himself to the town hall railings in protest at the Sunday licensing hours and the stage manager, thwarted in love, spread himself across the tram lines. These scandalous happenings, followed by a production of *The Beaver Coat*, a play translated from the German and delivered in a Lancashire accent, brought about the sudden dismissal of the producer, whereupon, out of loyalty, myself and another actor promptly gave in our notice. Neither of us had any money and had to hide in a cottage beneath the Tay bridge until funds arrived and we could buy train tickets. I returned to Liverpool and got married to the young artist I had first met when he painted scenery at the Liverpool Playhouse.

It was not entirely the end of my acting career, for in 1960, about the same time as the publication of the unabridged version of *Lady Chatterley's Lover* – it was passed from hand to hand during rehearsals – I played Ken Barlow's girlfriend, or rather one of his fellow students, in an episode of *Coronation Street*. The action involved us being ticked off by his mother for making a mess of her living room while making placards for Ban the Bomb. Cherie Booth's father was in the same episode, and together we travelled by train to the studios in Manchester. Those were the days when the carriages were crowded with what my Dad brutally referred to as 'White Trash', meaning young girls bound for Warrington and the American air-force base. The rejects, coming home at night, unscrewed the light bulbs and wept in the darkness.

That was all a long time ago, and I cannot say that such theatrical experiences were of much use to me when it came to reviewing. Indeed, I fear the reverse was the case, for I've found it impossible to condemn out of hand anything I've seen in the last eleven years. Alas, I'm too conscious of the hopes, the money and the effort that goes into each production.

On re-reading my so-called criticisms I'm astonished to find that in the early years I relied heavily on a book called *An Actor's Craft* published in 1930 and written by one Herbert Jennings. Recently, fetching it down from the shelves and blowing off the dust, I was intrigued by the numerous photographs of Mr Jennings' distorted face illustrating such conflicting emotions as determination, indignation, perplexity, surprise and fury. The last image, with its bulging eyes and bared teeth is truly frightening. There's an even worse one depicting madness, in which Jennings' hair has gone mad too.

As an example of his style, and advice, here is Mr J. on assessing the part of a King: 'In the impersonation of a monarch it is more than probable that an uncultured ploughman attempting the role will lamentably fail if he merely follows his imagination, whilst it will be just as difficult for a King to pass himself off as a rustic.'

And on facial expression: 'Dramatic history records that Mlle Clairon sat down in an easy chair and without saying a word or making a single gesture, she depicted upon her face alone, hatred, rage, indignation, indifference, sadness, love, pity, indolence, joy, etc.'

And on how best to express violent or sudden grief: 'The whole attitude should become uncontrolled and pass into a physical condition. The voice rises rapidly in pitch and we hear violent weeping, screaming, a hurrying to and fro and the rending of hair and garments by the distracted person. Tears do not always flow, but the nostrils are often widely extended.'

I suppose we should be grateful that this robust style of acting has gone out of fashion, and that audiences viewing the more subtle performances of today no longer have cause to cry out in terror. Nor do we react in quite the same way to productions we dislike.

In 1754, the great actor manager David Garrick brought over a hundred Frenchman to perform in an elaborate kind of ballet entitled *A Chinese Festival*. The political climate in Europe was edgy; the Seven Years War which would pit England against France was imminent. On the first night at Drury Lane fighting broke out; rotten apples deluged the stage. Unrest continued for several nights, reaching a climax on the 18th of November when 'The rioters tore up the benches and threw them into the pit onto the opposing party; they broke all the mirrors, the chandeliers etc.; and tried to climb onto the stage to massacre everybody; but as there is a magnificent organisation in this theatre, in three minutes all the decor had been removed, all the traps were ready to come into play to swallow up those who might venture up, all the wings were filled with men armed with sticks, swords, halberds etc.; and behind the scenes the great reservoir was ready to be opened to drown those who might fall on the stage itself.'

Modern attitudes to theatre – think of the tame response to Jerry Springer – are possibly due to the invention of television. Nightly we are subjected to visual images of slaughter and mayhem. At the moment, all four soaps – *Emmerdale, Coronation Street, EastEnders* and *Neighbours* – have storylines involving murder. It could be argued that Shakespeare favoured much the same content, but then, he was a master of his craft.

In the old days a visit to the theatre had a certain magic; one entered a world of make-believe. At Liverpool two pianists sat in the pit and tinkled away on the ivories until the house lights began to fade. Footlights required the actors to wear heavy make-up; a velvet curtain swished apart to reveal the set; the sound of thunder was made by rattling a length of tin. Oh, the poignancy of it! Now, the stage is open to view on entering the auditorium. Sometimes the actors stroll around as if the play had already begun. There's no curtain to hush one into silent anticipation, merely that disembodied voice urging the disconnection of mobile phones. Yet still the magic shines through. With few exceptions the plays that I have reviewed in the last decade remain in my mind, both for the quality of the construction and the brilliance of the performances.

At the time of writing this introduction there are no less than eighteen musicals being staged in London theatres. In regard to this kind of entertainment, who better to express my feelings than Mr Jennings: 'It is not intended that a musical play should be taken seriously. Fun and frolic, catchy airs and seductive symphonies must take the place of the serious sentiment and sensational situations of a dramatic production.'

# 1992

Death of Benny Hill, Frankie Howerd, Marlene Dietrich, Denholm Elliot, Robert Morley and the last survivor of the *Titanic*, Marjorie Robb.

Windsor castle caught fire.

The US spaceship *Endeavour* carried the first married couple into space. They were of different sexes.

My play *An Awfully Big Adventure* was performed at the Liverpool Playhouse with my daughter, Rudi Davies, playing me. Ronnie Settle came back to play the piano, but alas, the footlights had gone for ever.

# The Wind in the Willows

## National Theatre, 21 February 1992

It is sensible when embarking on a new enterprise to state one's intentions. Such openness can go some way towards unravelling later misunderstandings. In my opinion reviewers are regrettably dependent on personality; they see what they have been taught to see, they think the way they have always thought. In order to combat this insularity of perception I intend to rely heavily on Herbert Jennings, author of that classic work *An Actor's Craft*. It was H. J., you will remember, who, paraphrasing Chaucer's dictum that an actor should 'make his English sweet upon the tongue', observed how fond we are of a melodious voice, and that, following hard on the heels of Dramatic Expression, the purpose of the Theatre is to make Good the Word.

Bearing his remarks in mind, I set off to see *The Wind in the Willows* at the National Theatre. As you will doubtless know, this is a sinister and psychological work, admirably adapted this time by Alan Bennett from a book by Kenneth Grahame, about three bachelors, Ratty, Mole and Badger, who are determined to subdue a fourth, the life-enhancing and admittedly unstable Mr Toad. It's sort of Brecht with the sun shining.

I had heard that there was a whiff of homosexuality about the production, but I found no evidence of this, and though it was perhaps a little foolish of Moley to be picked up quite so quickly on the riverbank, one had only to watch the way Ratty wriggled with pleasure when the washerwoman's daughter kissed him to realize the absurdity of such an imputation. Mr Bennett has been true to the book and there was, as befits the golden age in which the play is set,

11

a lot of sunshine. Perhaps therein lies the rub. I felt the Wild Wood could have been darker. Doesn't anyone out there remember a fear of the dark?

All in all, I felt the 'magic' of the theatre was absent, an absence due not to a lack of clarity of Word or melodiousness of Voice on behalf of writer or actors – the sound of the hoofs of Albert the Horse as he plodded round the riverbank was acting of the highest calibre – but rather to an insane presumption by directors that an audience should be part of a production. I refer, of course, to the potty abolition of wings, curtain, proscenium arch, footlights and dimming of the house. I was forced to smile throughout, facial muscles stuck in a grimace owing to the brightness of the auditorium.

Surely the point of a theatrical experience is that we should be cut off from it, left out, yet wanting to be part of it, aching to will Moley's nose to sniff out his lost home, so that when he finds it we break out into applause stimulated by affection rather than astonishment at the technical chicanery of scenery whirring up, down and sideways.

One last thought. Why couldn't we have Pavarotti on Moley's gramophone belting out *Bless This House* instead of all those children dressed up as bunnies? And why didn't Moley drop to his knees, expressing joy at being home? I was worried why the kiddies weren't in bed, and besides, they couldn't make enough noise. As H. Jennings once wrote: 'The most simple effects are usually the most striking. Have you not often seen a little girl of an emotional temperament hugging her breast with her forearms in a state of ecstatic anticipation, or a person kneeling in sudden adoration or excessive devotion or humility?'

# Faith Healer

## 6 March 1992

There's a very good anecdote attributed to Claud Cockburn in the programme notes of the play *Faith Healer* by Brian Friel. Cockburn, newly arrived in summer to live in Ireland, and observing the way the constant rain turned into mist, remarked to a neighbour how little could be seen through the haze. To which his listener, anxious to be responsive replied, 'Ah, surr, it's the hate.'

The same telling shifting of meaning can occur when an Irish voice pronounces the word faith and turns it into fate. Faith, particularly when applied to the Catholic religion, can move mountains, whereas fate, like Mount Everest, is fixed and unchangeable. That which is destined to happen will happen, or as Doris Day so ably warbled, *Qué sera sera.*

Interesting as this somewhat metaphysical digression may be, it has sweet F-all to do with the play. Although fate is ever present, there is far more love than haze.

*Faith Healer* is a superbly constructed drama consisting of four monologues, the first and last spoken by Frank the Healer, the second by his wife, Grace, and the third by Teddy, his show business manager. Scenery is minimal, and there is little physical movement except when one or other of the protagonists lights up a fag or pours another drink.

The monologues dwell on the past, and two events in particular, the death of Frank in the yard of a pub in Ireland and Grace giving birth to a still-born child in the back of a van at the side of a road outside Sunderland. Grace's version of this latter event is touching and verging on the poetic. The infant was shovelled into a grave under a hedgerow in a field; Frank made a small cross and spoke comforting words; the cows looked on, munching. Teddy's version is more brutal. When Grace went into labour Frank legged it off up the hill and didn't come back until it was all over and Teddy had buried the child. It was Teddy, not Frank, who fashioned the cross and uttered the appropriate words. Frank remarks that he would have wished for a child, but Grace was barren. He mentions the road outside Sunderland and falls silent mid-sentence.

For once, that theatrical cliché, 'he dominates the stage', comes into its own, for Donal McCann in the title role gives a magnificent performance. Shoulders hunched in his shabby suit, he's the charming bounder and lost boy.

Ron Cook, who plays his manager, is equally brilliant. 'Dear heart, the man knew what he was doing,' he cries as, wandering about his bed-sit, he leads us to the final scene in that pub yard in Ireland.

The story is as follows: Frank, Grace and Teddy travel around the British Isles, to obscure venues in dilapidated church halls, to heal the sick. Frank knows when he can heal somebody. Mostly he doesn't – heal them, that is – but there are occasions when he's flooded with power. One such happening takes place in a village in Glamorganshire. Ten people, the halting and the blind, became whole again.

After this triumph, it's all downhill. He returns to Ireland and one night in a pub meets a group of unbelievers, one of whom has a finger curled up on account of severed tendons. Taking the damaged digit between his palms, Frank restores it to mobility, and straightens out his own life. Everybody's drunk, and the men go to fetch a friend who's confined to a wheelchair. Frank knows he won't be able to heal him. He also knows that when he fails he'll be battered to death.

A lesser playwright would have the cripple dance from his chair. The tension, without which dramatic movement is inhibited, much like a damaged tendon, is sustained throughout. It's a wonderful play, beautifully acted. The staging and direction are in keeping with it. The audience sat in pitch darkness, watching, unseen, sniffing a bit.

Herbert Jennings, author of that seminal work *An Actor's Craft*, wrote that it was no duty of a critic of the drama to divulge the plot. In this particular instance I feel I may be excused for dwelling so long on the story. By the time you read this the play will have come off.

# Henry IV, Part II
## 15 May 1992

Herbert Jennings wrote that familiarity with Shakespeare's work neither 'stales our delight in it nor reduces our wonder at its variety; for our amazement at the seventh perform-ance of *Hamlet* is greater than it was at the first. We can grasp the contents of a penny paper at one glance, but must look often into the writings of great men before we begin to understand all that they have to tell us.' Correct as he undoubtedly was, I don't think I could sit through *Henry IV, Part II* more than twice. I suspect I don't like comedy, at least not of the Shakespearean kind, and much prefer the great man when he's preoccupied with failure and madness.

Though I did enjoy in some measure the performance of *Henry IV, Part II* at the Barbican Theatre, with the excep-tion of the death of the King and Doll's declaration of love for Falstaff, I remained an unmoved onlooker throughout. (Actually, that's not quite true, for in the middle of the second half of the play I got a fit of coughing and, in an effort to suppress it, nearly choked to death and had to go out for quarter of an hour. Fortunately the Barbican pro-vides a room for the dying, equipped with closed-circuit television. It was very odd heaving and wheezing while watching the King expiring in an equally dramatic fight for breath.)

For those few of you not familiar with the plot of *Henry IV, Parts I* and *II*, time follows on from the betrayal and removal to the tower of Richard II. Bolingbroke, usurper of Richard, seizes the throne and becomes Henry IV. In *Part II*, he's dying. His son and heir to the throne, Hal, is no good and spends all his time in a Gloucester brothel, in company with a recruiting officer called Falstaff who has a terrible friend, Pistol, an elderly version of a Chippendale boy who sports an erect, black willie and is always breaking up the furniture. It's in this dolls' house of ill-repute – the set is responsible for the pun, not I – run by Mistress Quickly, that a scene of painful tenderness is enacted between Fatty Falstaff and the no-better-than-she-should-be Doll. Cradling his wobbling jowls in her hands, she cries hoarsely, 'I love you'.

Such is the superbly relaxed performance of Robert Stephens as the rollicking and corrupt Falstaff, that one finds nothing perverted in her passion for this ruin of a man. I think he loved Doll too, though he was obviously sleeping with Mistress Quickly. The fact that I was more interested in this sub-plot than in the wider political ramifications of the text supports my own personal view that the play doesn't work. Ostensibly, it's about the importance of succession, yet in the end we only remember death, love and Falstaff getting his comeuppance at the coronation. Informed that Henry IV has died and that Hal, alias Henry V, has seized the crown, Falstaff believes he is in a position of power and in sight of solvency. 'My sweet boy,' he cries out, as the newly crowned King passes in procession. 'I know you not,' responds his sovereign, having unaccountably turned over a new leaf and forsworn his dissolute ways, whereupon Fatty sinks to his knees.

Julian Glover, as the dying King, was excellent. He mouthed his words with passion and coughed his life out with conviction. I believed he was dying, though I wasn't at all certain that the grief shown by his son, young Hal, was genuine. His conversion, his sudden abhorrence of brothels and old soldiers, struck a false note. Surely one can't alter the habits of a lifetime.

It's strange that watching a great company perform a play

brilliantly directed and staged in a huge theatre to an auditorium packed to the rafters should still leave one empty, as though excellence was at war with involvement. But judging by the storm of applause at the end, I was the odd woman out.

PS. A Chippendale boy is a reference to a troupe of young men who sing and gyrate in nothing other than G-strings.

# An *Awfully Big Adventure*

## Liverpool Playhouse, 3 April 1992

It was Herbert Jennings, I think, who held that the romantic experiences of actors and actresses, as well as of authors and patrons of the stage, have provided material for many a novelist's plot. Yet despite this we can hardly now comprehend the depths of privation to which these people often sank, nor the iron curtain of contempt and insult behind which they so constantly laboured.

*An Awfully Big Adventure* is a play about such contemptibles. The time is 1950, a mere twenty years before the demise of the repertory system, that golden time when every city in England still supported a permanent theatrical company. Actors then were expected to dress like ladies and gentlemen and received a pittance in wages, as well as being required to affect what was referred to by the rest of us as lah-de-dah voices. This was taken for granted, just as it was accepted that both cast and audience should smoke their heads off throughout the performance. Backstage a fireman with a bucket ran after the actors as they marched up and down in the wings.

This is the world in which *An Awfully Big Adventure* is set. The plot is deceptively simple. A young girl, Stella, is taken on as general dogsbody. The play in rehearsal is *Peter Pan*, that sinister combination of feckless mothers, lost boys and Mr Darling, whose careless banishment of Nanny from the nursery opens the window to Never Never Land. It's no accident that Darling and his alter-ego, the devilish Captain Hook, are traditionally performed by the same actor.

There's something dark in Stella's background, something nasty in the woodshed. She has an aversion to night-lights, to the smell of candle-grease. She telephones her mother constantly. Almost immediately she falls in love with Potter, the theatre director. Discussing a previous production, Priestley's *Dangerous Corner*, he asks Stella what she thinks the play is about. 'Love,' she replies promptly. 'People loving people who love somebody else.' 'No,' he tells her. 'Mostly it has to do with Time. Think of it this way. . . . We are mourners following a funeral procession, and some of us, those of us more directly concerned with the departed, have dropped behind to tie a shoelace. Contact with the beloved is only temporarily interrupted . . . the dead are still there, as are those we think we love.'

In this web of words and make-believe, Stella's innocence is dangerous. Her candour causes upsets, physical as well as emotional; there is an attempted suicide; the leading man falls and breaks his leg, necessitating the arrival of another actor to take over the role of Captain Hook. I can't tell you the rest of the plot, but sufficient to say it's a bit like an onion and has many skins. The actors are all wonderful and play as a team. The set is imaginative and the lighting magical, though after the preview the machinery working the revolve blew up and it had to be pushed round manually for a night or two. This didn't really matter except that in the seduction scene Captain Hook had to take his trousers off in slow motion.

Too much of the first act is given over to exposition. There must be a better way of doing it. Given time, the author may write a better play. As Stella says in the closing moments before the curtain falls: 'I wasn't the only one at fault. I'll know how to behave next time . . . I'm learning.'

# The Blue Angel

Globe Theatre, Shaftesbury Avenue, 29 May 1992

It's impossible to sit through Pam Gems' stunning adaptation of *The Blue Angel*, now showing at the Globe Theatre, Shaftesbury Avenue, without heaving with nostalgia. Why is it that countries so close together, geographically speaking, produce such diverse yet nationally recognizable forms of artistic expression? Why, apart from the fact that they all spoke the mother tongue, do we perceive Marie Lloyd, Turner and Joe Orton as English? For what reason – apart from the cold – did Norway and Sweden throw up Ibsen, Strindberg, and Amundsen, for that matter? It can't all be put down to an accident of birth. Why did the French produce Monet, Manet, Molière, M Hulot and the can-can? And why is it that the creative work of Germans of a certain period stinks of decadence?

Heinrich Mann, brother of the more illustrious Thomas, wrote a number of satirical novels knocking the society and institutions of Wilhelminian Germany. It's a shock to read in the programme notes that he only died in 1950. To me that's yesterday.

*Professor Unrath*, his poetic novel – since labelled, for what it's worth, as neo-romantic – was published in 1905 and picked up 25 years later by the director Josef von Sternberg. He turned it into *The Blue Angel*, a film which might have sunk without trace if he hadn't added the ingredient of cabaret and cast an unknown girl called Marlene Dietrich in the role of Lola.

The story is common enough for the time: a pompous professor (here called Professor Raat) falls for night-club

singer, marries her, loses his position in society and evades
financial ruin by becoming a pimp and a blackmailer.

It's easy for a mere onlooker to attribute the success of a
drama to the actors. If the set is satisfactory one can forget
the lighting and the direction and remember only the
stance and voices of those cavorting about the stage. In this
particular production, there isn't one bum performer, and
the lighting is brilliant. The casting, of course, is down to
the director, Trevor Nunn, though I gather his Lola, Kelly
Hunter, wasn't his first choice.

I can't find enough superlatives to praise this actress. How
do we manage – we British, year after year – to come up
with these astonishing talents? Miss Hunter is a stick insect,
a moth-pale, gawky, beautiful girl who struts about the set
in suspenders and not much else, and yet isn't embarrassing.
Her Lola is corrupt, damaged – I got the impression her dad
was more loving than he should be – and her careless
warmth towards Professor Raat strikes exactly the right
note. It isn't that Lola can't feel love; as a realist, she knows
that passion isn't often reciprocated.

Philip Madoc, as the Professor, is equally good. In the
middle, when his students discover he's hopelessly infatuated with Lola, he comes over as a dead ringer for that
house-master in *Goodbye Mr Chips*. He's vulnerable, as he
should be. Like Mr Chips, he's a bigot, in that he believes in
the Establishment. Unlike Mr Chips, who in the end passed
on in a jelly of sentimentality, Raat dies because his heart
can't stand the quickened pace.

What else? I liked the chubby bathing belles wobbling
nightly at the Blue Angel, the clown, the master of cere-
monies, his wife and daughter, the Baron who lusts after
Lola and who, true to his class, will never make her his wife.

The final image is of Lola straddling a chair and singing
'*Ich Bin von Kopf Bis Fuss auf Liebe Eingestellt*' – in other

words, 'Falling in Love Again'. That she never wanted to goes without saying.

See the play ye oldies. You'll find it familiar. Ye youngies will surely burst into tears.

# The Woman in Black

## Fortune Theatre, 12 June 1992

*The Woman in Black*, currently in performance at the Fortune Theatre, is a ghost story. I think it's set in that time before the War when all gentlemen wore waistcoats. Mr Arthur Kipps, now well into the middle ground of age, is haunted by an experience which took place in his youth, when, as a young solicitor, he was sent to the misty North to sort out the affairs of the deceased Mrs Drablow, an elderly recluse who lived in a house which could only be reached by a causeway when the tide went out.

Mr Kipps, in order to exorcize the past, writes down his story and pays a young actor to bring it to dramatic life. We see the two of them, in three successive days, rehearsing a production that may eventually be seen only by family and friends of the unhappy author. Actually, Mr Kipps no longer has a family (the Woman in Black put paid to his wife and child).

In the first act, the stage is bare save for a theatrical skip, later to do duty as the interior of a puff-puff train and the exterior of a horse and cart, a metal clothes rack hung with various coats and scarves, an invisible small dog called Spider, a couple of chairs, and a backcloth seen through a gauze of sheets piled in tombstone shapes to represent a graveyard.

No one will talk to the young Mr Kipps about his dead client, Mrs Drablow. Not Mr Keckwick, the pony-and-trap man, Mr Daily, the agent, nor the waiter in the hotel. Nor will any of them answer his queries as to the identity of the cadaver-faced lady flitting about the graveyard.

It's not a great play and the device of a play within a play is not structurally satisfying. It's not *Henry IV Part I,* or even *II* – one is tempted to remark that this is all to the good – but it is a cracking night out. 'Recite it like that,' the young actor instructs Mr Kipps as he laboriously reads out his part, 'and you'll send your audience to sleep.' If this was any other play, he'd be on tricky ground.

As it is, sleep is the last thing on our minds when Mr Kipps stays in the haunted house with Spider. He also behaves as you or I would, and not at all like those irritating protagonists in horror films who, fully cognizant of something nasty in the woodshed, possibly killer bees, unaccountably rush towards the hive. Spider, closely followed by Mr Kipps, very sensibly runs at the speed of light in the opposite direction.

Stephen Mallatratt, who adapted the play from the novel by Susan Hill, has done a masterly job, topped by its director, Robin Herford of the Stephen Joseph Theatre at Scarborough. If I don't mention Milton Johns as Mr Kipps, or the actor Steven Mackintosh, it's because I forgot they were acting.

I came home in a taxi driven by a chap who had already seen the play. He'd enjoyed it so much he'd recommended it to his parents and then his in-laws. He knew far more about it than I did. Did I know that the man playing Kipps was Brendan Scott in *Coronation Street*?

There's a moment in the second act of *The Woman in Black* when something unspeakable happens. I shan't tell you what it is. I was seated between a stranger and Mr Ingrams, editor of *The Oldie.* Sufficient to say that at the moment of ultimate horror both Mr Ingrams and the stranger underwent minor heart attacks. I didn't feel too chipper myself.

Oddly enough, half an hour later I experienced what can only be called elation. No wonder *The Woman in Black* has been running for years. What the man on the Clapham omnibus with an Old Age Pensioner's pass requires is to be taken out of himself. Life being what it is and all things being equal, it's rather refreshing to jump out of one's skin.

# *Déjà vu*

## Comedy Theatre, 26 June 1992

John Osborne's play, *Déjà vu*, now showing at the Comedy Theatre, is a mess, yet in parts it is better than anything else on at the moment. Taking it in is a bit like an act of faith.

It's too long, too wordy, and the now middle-aged Jimmy Porter is too fond of sashaying to the gramophone to put on an old-time melody whenever he wants to manipulate the audience. I suspect the failure of the play to be moving lies mainly in the casting of Peter Egan as Jimmy. He's just too nice to portray that swine Porter. I suspect that the director was swayed by Egan's superb portrayal of Oscar Wilde, and it is true that the play comes alive whenever Jimmy gyrates his pelvis. But there's no way someone with eyes like that could ignore his children and stamp on their transistors.

I don't think it's necessary to have seen *Look Back in Anger* (I hadn't), nor does it matter that I missed the significance of the ironing board, or Teddy for that matter. I think there's a limit to the symbolic importance of an ironing board. As for Teddy, I have a tailor's dummy in my living-room, dressed up as Neville Chamberlain, with whom I often bandy words. I reckon both Teddy and Neville are perfectly clear symbolic representations of childhood – one cuddly, if a little sinister when one thinks of the song about going down to the woods at night for a picnic; the other redolent of 'Peace in our Time', surely something all children have access to, along with cod liver oil and Marmite sandwiches. (There's an amusing bit in the first act when Porter, riffling through the Sunday papers, comes across *The Oldie*. 'Oh God,' he cries, flinging it away in disgust. I expect he went and read it in the interval.)

The young person who accompanied me to the matinée had seen the film *Look Back in Anger* with Richard Burton as the lead. She said the young Jimmy, however angry, was full of love and 'activated' by pain. She doesn't read *The Spectator, Private Eye* or *The Oldie* and, as yet, isn't blunted enough to appreciate irony. In her opinion, the middle-aged Jimmy is a racist, a fascist, a gay-basher, in short a 'guy' full of hatred. All this, despite the fact that the character, accused of just such callousness by his own daughter, goes to some lengths to explain that anger, springing from a sense of loss, is too sad to contain hate.

During the interval, my companion declared that the old Jimmy wasn't really angry, just incapable of keeping his mouth shut. Furthermore, he wasn't offensive because he was no longer dangerous. Having cut off his nose to spite his face, he'd suffered a severing of the arteries (I queried this on medical grounds), had stopped bleeding and was merely dying.

At this, an American lady, waving her hands to disperse my ciggie smoke, shook on her stool. 'You think he did something when he went to answer the phone?' she asked. 'Is that why he came back so pale?'

In 1959, when Errol Flynn and Buddy Holly died and Supermac and Castro swept into power, Tom Maschler edited *Declaration*, a compilation of 'statements' by novelists, critics and dramatists. In it, Kenneth Tynan wrote:

A play is an ordered sequence of events that brings one or more of the people in it to a desperate condition, which it must always explain and if possible resolve. If the worst that can happen is the hero's being sent down from Oxford, we laugh and the play is a farce; if death is a possibility, we are getting close to tragedy. Where there is no desperation, or where the desperation is inadequately motivated, there is no drama; characters, for instance, who scream when their noses are tickled or commit suicide the day after falling in love are bad cases of inadequately motivated desperation. These broad rules apply not only to all successful drama from Aristophanes to Beckett, but also to the narrative arts of novel and film.

In the same book, young Osborne writes:

I can't go on laughing at the idiocies of the people who rule our lives. We have been laughing at their gay little mad-nesses, my dear, at their point to points, at the postural slump of the well-off and mentally underprivileged, at their stoop-ing shoulders and strained accents, at their waffling cant, for too long. They are no longer funny, because they are not merely dangerous, they are murderous. . . . It is an inescapable fact that when the middle class discuss experience that is not dominated by their own emotional values, they hedge and bluster with all they've got.

Osborne hasn't changed, thank heavens. It's just that he no longer has faith in the young chaps who are prepared to direct his work. He should have cut his play. He should have had O'Toole, a born-again man if ever there was one, as Porter. It should never be forgotten that modern theatre proprietors don't allow their patrons to smoke. Watching a play has now become an exercise in self-denial, something Jimmy is still deeply into.

# *Improvizafond*

## Le Place de l'Horloge, Minerbes, 21 August 1992

The French do things superbly well, don't they? And it can't all be down to the weather. When one contrasts the final few days of the Avignon Festival with the vulgar opening spectacle of the Olympic Games, the mind boggles. In the past I've been to rather worthy piano recitals and the like, but this year I decided to go to a 'fringe' entertainment at a cinema in Le Place de l'Horloge just off the magnificent square of the Palais des Papes. The show was called *Improvizafond* and featured two young comedians somewhat similar in looks to our own Smith and Jones, though the French Smith looked healthier and the Jones was more like Jean Louis Barrault.

The show began at 10.30 at night, a barbaric enough hour were it not for the fact that everyone on the Continent goes to bo-bo's for the afternoon, and before we took our seats we were asked to write down the title of a small drama we wished to see enacted. My heart sank at this because I mistakenly thought we were in for two hours of unspeakably boring mime, but I obediently asked for the first encounter of Stanley and Livingstone in the jungle; more imaginatively, another of our party requested a scene between Princess Di and Charlie after that dreadful day when young Wills was cracked over the head by a playmate at school.

In the event, neither of our contributions were picked out of the hat, and for all of five minutes I was convinced – such was the inventiveness of the suggestions chosen and the brilliance of the comedians who interpreted them – that the entire evening was a subtle con-trick and that the dazzling performers, far from improvising, had rehearsed down to the last 'Ooh-la-la!' This notion was dispelled when the man in front of me nearly burst his braces with pride when Smith, alias Benjamin Rataud, though it may have been Jones, alias Phillippe Lelievre, read out that they would attempt to portray two sugar cubes about to enter two cups of tea . . . in the manner of Samuel Beckett.

There was a girl pianist who most eloquently accompanied the action, a coach, with whom the actors conferred before getting down to business, and a lighting man. I can't speak French, but I can read the headlines in *Figaro* and I do pick up the odd word when spoken with feeling, and though I can't pretend to have caught the jokes – I mean I didn't laugh – I did understand what it was about. One sugar cube was perched on its spoon; the other was in the bowl. This is how some of the dialogue went, more or less, though possibly less than more:

> 'C'est le moment, mon ami.' (Sigh)
>
> 'Quel est un moment. . . . C'est la question.' (Heavier sigh)
>
> 'Ah . . . toute la vie est un dissolvement . . .' (More cheerful – I think)
>
> 'Un moment je suis ici . . . le ciel se décoloré, et c'est une charme unique . . . bientôt, oblivion.'

There was also a subplot to do with a cousin called saccharine; the tea-drinker on the left was on a diet, and pour un moment the drinker on the right, sugar spoon dipping towards the cup, was swayed in favour of slimness. In the end, both threw caution to the winds and, babbling of sweetness, thrust the cubes into the liquid.

There followed a skit about an inept professor visited by a schools inspector. We, the audience, automatically fell into the role of students. 'Carry on as normal,' urged the inspector. Several naughty boys and girls screwed their programmes into aeronautical shapes and bombarded the stage with flying arrows. The professor begged for our attention. Everyone laughed a lot, but I missed why.

I almost got the next one, entitled 'The Man Who Married A Man'. In the hotel bedroom the bride goes for a pee and the groom creeps up on her. 'Mon Dieu,' he squeaks. 'What est that?'

> 'Mon petit Gadget,' the bride replies.
> 'How can I ever tell your mother?'
> 'She'll understand. She's mon père.'

We came out into the warm midnight to the sound of Bolivian musicians tramping round in a circle strumming banjos made in the Andes. The Palace des Papes was flood-lit. The birthday guests at a long table were smiling at an iced cake riddled with a hundred candles. The birthday girl, hitherto comatose in her wheelchair, stretched her bony arms to the sky before sliding to the ground. I suspect she was playing at being a sugar cube.

# *It Runs In The Family*

## Playhouse Theatre, 4 September 1992

I once played in that splendid farce, *Rookery Nook*, at the old Scala Theatre which used to stand in Tottenham Court Road and was impolitely known as the Dust Hole. The co-author of the play, Ben Travers, came to the rehearsal and a more morose-looking old gentleman one could not wish to meet. The plot is a little hazy after all these years, except that it involved lovely Peter Cushing and David Kossoff and that I was required to appear in pyjamas; there was also a lady who popped in and out in her underwear selling flags for the life-boat.

I do remember, however, taking my role very seriously and looking up the meaning of 'farce' in my trusty volume on stage lore written by Herbert Jennings. If my memory serves me right the Greeks started it all – long before Christ, there was a popular farcical character called Maccus, who invariably ended up dressed as a woman – and then the Italians and the French copied them.

The farce *It Runs In The Family*, by Ray Cooney, now showing at the Playhouse Theatre, is well worth seeing. I was taken by a woman friend who, anxious that I should enjoy the evening, looked sideways at me for signs of joviality long before the curtain went up. For the first few minutes – I now realize I suspend disbelief rather slowly – a fixed smile remained on my lips and a sliver of ice in my heart. My friend was already guffawing, so much so that the row in front turned round in alarm.

The set was a doctor's common-room in some hospital in the metropolis. Dr Mortimer is discovered pacing up and down rehearsing the Ponsenbury Lecture he will give in one hour's time to 300 delegates from overseas. If he pulls it off he will be elevated to head boy of the hospital, and then possibly to knighthood. Enter a busty young blonde in a scarlet dress whom he last saw when he was rolling about with her in the sluice room 19 years before. The offspring of their coupling is downstairs in reception in an unstable state demanding to be told who Daddy is. Enter Dr Mortimer's supportive wife, followed by his 'Robertson Hare' colleague, Dr Bonney. In the next 60 seconds, Dr Mortimer, in a frantic attempt to hide his past, begins to spin that tangled web of deceit which in real life leads to strangulation and in farce to a better understanding.

I wish I knew what caused laughter. I know about fright and how if you're chased by a bull a chemical release of adrenaline will catapult you over a five-barred gate or up a tree, but where does that heaving, that side-splitting loss of control come from?

And why is a funny play generally considered to be of less import than a tragedy? After all, we know from our experience that the youth who's been fatherless and lied to for so long is irreparably damaged, just as we know that the apparently complacent wife, seduced nurse and used colleague must be suppressing hideous feelings of rejection, betrayal and hostility.

The cast are excellent and have served long apprenticeships; Doris Hare is luminous and not a day under 80 and Henry Kee, considerably younger, gives a brilliant, toothless and mouth-champing performance. In particular I liked young William Harry as Leslie. He knows about timing and in spite of his punk haircut he came over as lovable.

I felt weak afterwards and could have done with an injection of glucose. As for my friend, she laughed so much she announced she'd had a little accident.

# 1993

Death of Lilian Gish, Audrey Hepburn, Stewart Granger, Anthony Burgess, Cyril Cusack, Raymond Burr, Vincent Price, Rudolf Nureyev and footballer Danny Blanchflower.

Nelson Mandela won the Nobel Peace Prize.

An IRA bomb planted in a chip shop in Belfast killed nine people.

*Wallenstein* by Friedrich von Schiller is a play about a man who made a lot of money out of land deals and war-surplus goods during the first half of the Thirty Years War. He turned over a new leaf and tried to become a good man, only he left it too late and was assassinated.

# Medea

## Wyndham's Theatre, 7 January 1993

Anyone who wants to understand Greek tragedy should read Hugh Lloyd-Jones's collection of essays entitled *Blood for the Ghosts*, particularly the one on Nietzsche in which the dead philosopher's views are lucidly and marvellously expounded.

It was Nietzsche, not Freud (that shrinking Jewish boy), who saw the necessity to invent the concept of sublimation; he regarded the ancient gods as totem poles erected to portray the fearful realities of a universe in which mankind had no special privileges.

For him, what gave the tragic hero the chance to display his heroism against dreadful and irrational forces was the certainty of annihilation; and tragedy played out on the stage gave its audience comfort, not by purging their emotions but by bringing them face to face with the most awful truths of human existence.

Long before the action begins, irrational forces have shaped the life of Medea, heroine of Euripides' play now showing at the Wyndham's Theatre. Jason, the father of her children, has abandoned his family in order to make an advantageous marriage to King Creon's daughter; she is now under threat of banishment from Corinth.

'She will not eat; she lies collapsed in agony, dissolving the long hours in tears', observes the Nurse. It's not that Medea is a shrinking violet unable to cope on her own. It's true that she's an exile from her own country, but only because, mad with love for Jason, she connived at murder and was forced to flee. Bereft of his love, it's anger, not grief, that tears her apart. That she's mad and bad is obvious; the

37

slaughter of her children is not undertaken in a sudden fit of insanity, but coldly plotted to cause Jason maximum suffering and remorse.

This is a superb production much aided by the excellent sets and the performances of everyone concerned. Tim Woodward as Jason is clever and moving. Jason is an ambitious swine, well used to bloodshed, and yet, faced with the unnatural deaths of his children he manages to make us feel pity for him. Here is a man, one tells oneself, who might have turned out better if he'd only had the love of a good woman.

Diana Rigg has a magical theatrical presence and tremendous vocal ability. I think her voice, in its range and power, is superior to any other classical actress. Some critics found her performance as Medea brilliant, yet unmoving. I suspect this is because they wanted her to reduce them to tears at the contemplation of her wickedness.

The point is, Medea would have had to feel she was bad in order to make the rest of us more comfortable in our minds. And she didn't. Right to the end she never let up. Jason was the guilty one, Jason was at fault.

I'm basically on her side, though I think I may have pretended to have killed the children rather than have actually done it. But then, I'm a post-Freudian woman and the dubious product of a Christian upbringing.

Medea's last words to Jason are totally unforgiving:

*Would God I had not bred them,*
*Or ever lived to see*
*Them dead, you their destroyer!*

# Sunset Boulevard

## Adelphi Theatre, 3 September 1993

I often fall asleep listening to the wireless, so I hear snatches of the World Service in my dreams. The other night I heard some critic mumbling away about Gloria Swanson and Billy Wilder and how 'it' or 'he' didn't really get going until after the interval.

Billy Wilder, for those few who may be unacquainted with the name, is the great man who directed and co-scripted such magnificent films as *The Lost Weekend, Double Indemnity, Some Like It Hot* and *Sunset Boulevard*. The latter classic, in which Gloria Swanson played an ageing movie star descending into madness, was originally conceived by Wilder as an astringent satire on Hollywood. He wanted Mae West and Montgomery Clift in the leading roles. But Miss West refused the part and Clift dropped out two weeks before shooting was scheduled to begin. I saw the film a long time ago on television, and remember William Holden more than Gloria Swanson.

*Sunset Boulevard* can now be seen as an Andrew Lloyd Webber musical, directed by Trevor Nunn at the Adelphi Theatre, with book and lyrics by Christopher Hampton and Don Black. The overture is very loud, very lush, and one of the tunes is sort of swoony. Then the curtain rises, and Joe, the narrator tells us about himself. He's known in Hollywood, has plenty of friends, but no one wants his scripts and he hasn't any money. I suspect he has a drink problem. Holden, in the part, seemed intelligent and a bit weary. Kevin Anderson just seems young and curiously cross about something. Anyway, he lands up, by accident, outside this huge mansion on Sunset Boulevard, home of Norma

Desmond, forgotten darling of the silent screen, who is looked after by the faithful Max Von Mayerling, once her movie director and first husband, now functioning as butler-cum-chauffeur and gloriously attired in a Gestapo uniform.

I sat slumped for 15 minutes, deafened by noise, watching and yet not taking it in. And then, somewhere about the time when Max takes Joe to the guest room and begins to sing 'The Greatest Star of All', I got that tingly feeling and sat up. Of course, the interior set of the mansion, designed by John Napier, is a masterpiece. But looks aren't everything. One has to care about people; there has to be something which tugs at the heart. *Sunset Boulevard* is a love story – Max loves Norma, Norma thinks she loves Joe, and Joe, actually, almost loves Norma back. I warmed to Joe. He made me believe he did wish her well.

Which brings me to the performance of Patti LuPone, who plays Norma. I think she's a great actress. My eyesight isn't as good as it was, so it wasn't just the final scene in which, almost bald and mad as a hatter, she comes down that giant staircase thinking she's meeting Mr de Mille, that moved me. She has real presence; she sends off waves of madness, and yet one doesn't lose patience with her. What the audience was privileged to watch here was great theatre, great spectacle.

# *Wallenstein*

## Barbican: The Pit Theatre, 15 October 1993

*Wallenstein* by Friedrich von Schiller, currently being performed at The Pit in the Barbican, is one of the best plays
I've ever seen. Originally designed to occupy two full
evenings in the theatre, this adaptation runs for a little over
three hours.

Schiller, born in 1759, was a friend of Goethe. Both were
determined to create 'a classical' German literature which
would put their native language on a cultural level with
other European tongues. Schiller based the character of
Wallenstein on a Bohemian nobleman who, having made
his fortune out of land deals and war surplus goods during
the first half of the Thirty Years War, became one of the
richest and most powerful men in Europe. Commander-in-
chief of the imperial Catholic forces, he was removed from
his post, largely through jealousy, and later reinstated. In
1633 he secretly negotiated with the Protestants to bring
the war to an end, but his motives were misunderstood
and he was assassinated a year later. To this day historians
disagree as to whether he was hero or villain. I say misunderstood rather than mistrusted, because this is a tragedy in
which, along with the other protagonists in the drama, the
onlooker is left to make his own judgement. With superb
confidence, Schiller lets Wallenstein remain an enigma.

The set is minimal – a circle of chairs suggesting a military conference, a map of Europe suspended from the
ceiling, a skylight and two doors. The cast consists of
numerous generals – one of them, Commander Gordon,
was an ancestor of my literary agent – all beautifully acted,
and three women; Wallenstein's weeping wife, wayward

daughter and persuasive sister-in-law, the latter majestically played by Barbara Jefford. Olivia Williams as the daughter is unusual; she's very real and rather awkward.

For me, the pivot of the show was Philip Voss as Octavio Piccolomini, the man responsible for Wallenstein's downfall. I didn't think he was a baddie; he only did what a man had to do. His son, Max, was lovely too, but then, Schiller made him up. That is not to say that Ken Bones, in the title role, didn't shine equally brightly – he has a wonderful voice – just that, being an enigma, one couldn't pin him down, and I was irritated that he didn't see they were out to get him.

I'm at a loss to explain exactly why I was so moved by the play, which is in blank verse (for God's sake). Perhaps it has something to do with childhood and learning poetry at school. It's words that do it. Nowadays, we're so used to seeing sentimental plays devoid of sentiment, so used to sitcoms, so surfeited on pap, that great drama jars one to the bone. Some time towards the end of the play, when Octavio Piccolomini is already out to trap him, Wallenstein declaims:

*Know there are moments in the life of man*
*When he stands closer than at other times*
*To the directing spirit of the world,*
*And may put question to his destiny.*

Now there's a word to conjure with – destiny, I mean. It explains why so grand a man went like a lamb to the slaughter.

# Separate Tables

## Albery Theatre, 29 October 1993

*Separate Tables* by Terence Rattigan, currently showing at the Albery Theatre, consists of two one-act plays set in a boarding house in Bournemouth, the first taking place during the winter of 1952, the second in the summer of 1954. For those like myself who think of the Fifties as ending yesterday, it is a shock to be faced with the attitudes prevailing among the assorted residents of the Beauregard Private Hotel. Unlike the superb *Deep Blue Sea*, which still comes over fresh as a daisy, *Separate Tables* has dated.

In the first play, *Table By The Window*, it is difficult to take seriously the plight of an apparently brilliant and intelligent man reduced to drunkenness and penury simply because his vain and brittle wife refused to let him get his leg over as often as he liked. Granted, her all too frequent 'headaches' resulted in his giving her a good hiding, for which intemperate behaviour he received a six-month term of imprisonment. But it's odd that he went on carrying a torch for her for the next 12 years. That sort of thing couldn't happen now, not if he was absolutely normal and there were no children to worry about. Only women carry on like that. Nor would he, unless a masochist, take her back knowing she was a drug addict and still none too keen on a tumble between the sheets. I think he goes on loving her because Rattigan was a homosexual and his better and worse feelings forced him to believe that devotion and punishment were superior to sex. He based the character of the wife on the fashion model, Jean Dawnay, whom he grew very fond of and whom he had met through the Oliviers. I don't know what happened to Miss Dawnay in real life, or

43

who it was who loved her so, but I tend to think he can't have been a hundred per cent red blooded. That being said, who is?

The plot of the second play, *Table Number Seven*, concerns a Major Pollock and a Miss Railton-Bell. He's pathetic and boring to begin with, dignified and touching at the end. She's shy and sexually inhibited to the point of imbecility. She's also subservient to her monstrous Mum; (there's a distinct similarity here to that wet girl who was a companion to some bullying old American biddy before becoming second wife to the equally bullying Max de Winter). Mum, after reading in the local newspaper that Major Pollock has been up in court for fumbling women in the local cinema, calls a meeting of the residents and demands his immediate removal from the Beauregard Hotel.

I won't give away what happens, just that the last scene is Rattigan at his best. Long silences, real tension, great theatre. The plot – the author was always generous in telling what inspired him – was based on a scandal which had touched, but happily not damaged, the life of Rattigan's hero, the great John Gielgud.

The acting is a bit of a puzzle. Rosemary Leach as monstrous Mum is wonderful. She's like a loose cannon shattering the decorum of that Bournemouth dining room. Kate O'Malley as Doreen, the maid, is a delight, as is Charlotte Cornwell, the efficient and balanced manageress; she performs the function of that policeman in Priestley's *An Inspector Calls*. I'm not sure about Peter Bowles, who plays both the rejected husband and poor old Major Pollock, any more than I'm sure about Patricia Hodge in the roles of the castrating wife and the feeble daughter. I've admired both of them in other parts, but I think they're playing either against character or class.

Ernest Clark was wholly there as the ever-optimistic Mr Fowler. What presence! He won't remember me, but 40 years ago he came backstage to the Playhouse to visit Rosamund Burns. I can still see his suit, his shoes, hear his voice echoing along that corridor lit by gaslight. Alas, we were destined to sit at separate tables.

# *Hysteria*

## Royal Court Theatre, 12 November 1993

In 1964, on the day I left Liverpool, my lodgers, Harry the Lion and Leah, an elderly Jewess, gave me a book entitled *The Interpretation of Dreams* by Sigmund Freud. They wrote on the fly-leaf, 'Till we meet in 20 years' time in the Kardomah Café, Bold Street.' Alas, both of the signatories died within a decade, Harry from a premature heart attack and Leah from a daily douching of undiluted Lysol following an act of sexual congress 40 years before.

I was reminded of Leah – 'Darling, I know the Greek word for the uterus, but I've had mine out and it hasn't cured my neurosis' – when I went to a matinée performance at the Royal Court Theatre of Terry Johnson's drama, *Hysteria*.

At first I was bemused by *Hysteria*. One minute it was very serious – it begins with a young, obviously troubled girl tapping on the French windows of Freud's Hampstead home – and the next Salvador Dali had popped in for tea and was prancing about in his combinations. People hid in cupboards, hurled their camiknickers through doors and wore Wellington boots as gloves. Freud, wearing a red mackintosh, his cancer-rotten jaw held up with a bandage tied atop in a ludicrous bow, posed beside a bicycle from whose crossbar dangled a blue hot-water bottle. Towards the very end the walls of that wonderful room in Hampstead flew up and away and the clock on the wall melted. Four women, two of them oldish, came on naked and trotted panic-stricken against a scudding sky.

The tie-up with Dali and surrealism is explained in the dialogue. Dali asks Freud if his paintings are any good, at which Freud damningly replies, 'In classic paintings I

46

look to the subconscious; in a surrealist painting for the conscious.' The farcical element only becomes clear when Freud refers to his having seen a performance of Ben Travers's play, *Rookery Nook*, that surrealistic and hysterical romp in which characters rush through French windows and girls in underclothes sell flags for the lifeboat. If I hadn't later read the text I would have missed the significance of the four naked women – Freud failed to get his sisters out of Germany and they died in concentration camps.

There's an awful lot going on in this stunning play, and the actors – Harold Goodman, Phoebe Nicolls, David de Keyser and Tim Potter – all give massively intelligent performances.

My friend Leah had no patience with Freud's claim that hysteria or obsessional behaviour was the consequence of sex/pleasure later transformed into guilt. In her case, neither sex nor pleasure came into it, only shock and a necessity to get rid of the germs.

# Mr Director

## 26 November 1993

Fay Weldon's play *Mr Director* was first shown at the Orange Tree Theatre ten years ago. The theme of the piece, that of the incarceration of disturbed juveniles in children's homes, is more relevant than ever. This week two children are on trial for the murder of a little boy in Liverpool.

In Miss Weldon's play, the foul-mouthed, sexually active and ragingly angry thirteen-year-old Debbie has finally reached the point of no return. A persistent absconder and an expensive recipient of the 'care' system, she must either be tamed or drugged up to the eyeballs in some sort of maximum security establishment for the young in years, if not in heart. It is perhaps a bit of a cheat that she is also regarded as intelligent. She's certainly brighter than her 'carers', the bigoted yet well-meaning Harry and the absurdly repressed Marion.

In an effort to solve the problem of Debbie once and for all, the manager of the home, the Mr Director of the title, clears out the gymnasium and installs a sensory deprivation unit, a womb-like contraption complete with umbilical pipes equipped to dispense liquid and flush out waste. It is, of course, a far more hygienic system than the one provided by Debbie's deprived and feckless progenitor.

I now come to a problem which I admit is personal, that of a dislike of theatre in the round. I just hate sitting in light and being aware of other people if I'm supposed to be watching a work of imagination. It says much for the power of Miss Weldon's dramatic structure that, in spite of this distracting illumination, I was on the edge of my seat for a good portion of the evening. I've read other reviews – most of them uncomplimentary – but they were all (surprise, surprise) written by men. None of them mentioned Debbie's dad. One might have thought she was an immaculate conception.

At first I was hostile to Paul Shelly's Mr Director, then I warmed to him. His solution to Debbie's problem might seem extreme, but then, the final solution is even more barbaric. He goes too fast though. All of them go too fast, except Harry. But I expect that's because there's so much that has to be said.

I think Miss Weldon should adapt the play for television, and intersperse footage of those videoed scenes of Bootle supermarket the day little James Bulger was abducted. Months ago, when the story first broke, I rang the *Sunday Times* and said I'd like to cover the trial. I don't want to any more. I don't believe you can blame children, any more than you can accuse them of being vehicles of the devil. Children are the sum total of their upbringing, the result of mistakes and influences.

Those oldies amongst us with children who, in spite of economic stability and educational advantages have failed to achieve happiness (silly word) must surely stand convicted of neglect. Women know this. Why the hell can't men acknowledge it?

# *Looking Through A Glass Onion*

## Criterion Theatre, 10 December 1993

I thought *Looking Through A Glass Onion*, showing at the Criterion Theatre, was a play. It's not. It's a monologue about the life of John Lennon interspersed with Beatles songs. That isn't to say that John Waters, the man who wrote, sings and performs it with his fellow narrator, Stewart D'Arrietta, isn't a good actor, let alone musician. As it happens, he's very good indeed, which is not so surprising when one realizes that in 1988 he won the Australian Film award for Best Actor. He looks like a sort of young Joss Ackland, six foot high with a superior expression on his face and a haircut half way between Anthony Hopkins in *The Silence of the Lambs* and Richard Burton in *Cleopatra*. Also, his Liverpool accent is perfect, and him an Australian.

I took the grandchildren. Notwithstanding the fact that their mother's babysitter was often one of the Fab Four (in those days Stuart Sutcliffe, not Ringo, bashed away on percussion) they were far from enthusiastic at the prospect. 'Who cares about John Lennon?' they scoffed as we entered the auditorium.

Fortunately, the rest of us did, although it's too clever a show and it goes too fast to bring the audience to its feet, as happened when I saw *Buddy*. I sensed a curious lack of participation, a withdrawal on behalf of the onlookers. This puzzled me, because John Waters and Stewart D'Arrietta, the latter on piano and keyboard, are exceptional performers. I swear I started most of the clapping.

Perhaps this reserve had something to do with the way the songs were broken off in mid-flow, to be replaced by narrative. Most of us were oldies and it was definitely disruptive, having been blasted into the firmament by electronic guitars and whatever, to be suddenly dropped earthwards by mere words. After all, Lennon was that most seductive of all beings, an uneducated, clever chap thrust into a position of power. It wasn't comfortable listening to him explaining, in what passes for poetry, about his Mam dying, his Aunt Mimi not understanding his childish rebellions, and the manner in which Yoko Ono tamed him. Most of all, it was nervy the way he waxed on about love and his assertion that posing for photographs with his member dangling was a cry for Peace.

In the interval I told Bertie and Charlie how their grandfather had taught the rudiments of drawing to the great John Lennon at Art School. Bertie was impressed. His eyes opened wider. He didn't know Lennon had been shot dead by a madman. Charlie looked shifty. He'd heard it all before and he didn't rate the music.

The second half was much the same as the first. I understand why. If you become interested in a subject, you want to do it justice. Dramatically, we should have heard the shot which gunned Lennon down. Truthfully, it wasn't necessary, but then the dictionary definition of 'theatrical' makes play of the artificial, affected and simulated histrionic effects of drama.

Going home, Bertie confided to the taxi-driver that his Granddad had shot John Lennon. I know what he means.

# She Stoops To Conquer

## Queen's Theatre, 24 December 1993

The Queen's Theatre is currently showing a production of Oliver Goldsmith's *She Stoops To Conquer*. This play, written by a man whose humorous pleasantries were often mistaken by his contemporaries for blundering stupidity, has been revived, on average, every three years for the last two centuries. I'm under the impression I played the part of the maid in a revival at the Liverpool Playhouse 40-odd years ago. I had but one utterance, 'Shall I bring the cherry brandy, sir?' (or some such line) and muffed it. Fresh from my elocution lessons at Mrs Ackerley's in Crane Hall and scarlet with embarrassment at being attired in a gown which scarcely covered my chests, I pronounced brandy with a long 'a'.

Months before Goldsmith wrote his lasting work, he published a short treatise entitled *Essay on the Theatre* in which he appeared to be debunking something loosely called Sentimental Comedy, a genre in which the characters were always presented as fools with hearts of gold. He was bent on Satire, something which disturbed the critics. As the plot of *She Stoops To Conquer* lacked consistency and, moreover, kept its audience in a continuous roar, they persuaded themselves that comedy had merely spilled over into farce.

We don't really know whether Goldsmith minded – probably not, given that he'd always lived from hand to mouth and now had a success on his hands. Cruelly enough, on the first night, when picked up in St James's Park and brought to the theatre in Covent Garden in the middle of the fifth act, he entered to a prolonged hissing. He was about to make a run for it when his friend Coleman cried out,

'Doctor, don't be afraid of a squib when we have been sitting these two hours on a keg of gunpowder.'

It's hard for us to know what the fuss was about, unless we're aware of the social conventions of the 18th century. Shakespeare's genius transcends time, but it would be unprofitable to present *She Stoops To Conquer* in modern dress. Not that the Queen's production made such a leap, just that I went home after the interval. True, my youngest daughter was 11 days late in giving birth, but I couldn't stand the shouting, the absurd contemporary posturings of the talented David Essex and the camp antics of Donald Sinden, an actor who once gave a superlative, unsurpassed rendering of Malvolio capering about in his cross garters. Only Miriam Margolyes as Mrs Hardcastle, covered in mud at the bottom of the garden, evoked pathos. We get tired, we who are growing old, of imitation. What we ask for in the end is truth.

Earlier in the week I went to see Woodrow Wyatt's *High Profiles* at the Kenneth More Theatre in Ilford. This is a clever, witty play about contemporary politics in which a naughty MP is waiting to hear whether he will be given a place in the cabinet. His children misbehave, his wife is having an affair, and he is having it off behind the sofa with his secretary. This is the stuff of real farce. Alas, you can't see it; the run has ended.

# 1994

Death of Eugene Ionesco, Joseph Cotton, John Osborne, Dinah Shore, Peter Cushing, Burt Lancaster, Dennis Potter, Jacqueline Kennedy and America's last hangman.

Britain's National Lottery starts.

Opening of the Channel Tunnel.

Discovery of Fred and Rosemary West's house of horror.

*Macbeth* by William Shakespeare is about a Scotsman who is told by witches that he will be King. Not willing to wait, he kills the reigning King, and then murders the wife and children of Macduff. Everyone blames Lady Macbeth.

# Macbeth

## Barbican Theatre, 4 February 1994

The foyer of the Barbican was packed to the gunnels at the matinee of *Macbeth* at the Barbican Theatre. The house holds 1,500, and a good three quarters of the audience was composed of school children, a quarter of whom sported moustaches (the boys, that is).

Something went wrong backstage and we weren't allowed into the auditorium until five to two. A ragged chorus of 'Why are we waiting' broke out and tailed off, doused by English teachers under the influence of Mr Major's new standards.

Once seated and encouraged by tannoy announcements of an imminent start, we all shut up. The glittering silver curtain parted, on came the witches with breasts and beards – or rather, up they went on a moving platform – and we were off to Scotland and into that dreadful tale of ambition and bloodshed.

It begins quite cheerfully, in spite of the thunder and lightning. One feels that Macbeth was quite a harmless chap until the witches cackled out their prophesies – and if he had kept the information to himself he might have gone into old age smiling at what might have been. As it is, he can't wait to tell the wife and thus seals his fate and that of those countless others who stand in his path.

I thought Jacobi excellent in the title role. His wife's taunting of him for being a coward was absolutely unjust. One really did think him fond of Duncan. And he did rouse pity at the end, when, old and broken, he cries out: 'And that which should accompany old age, / As honour, love, obedience, troops of friends, / I must not look to have.'

Even better, having had his moment of remorseful intro-spection he fairly charges back into wickedness. Damned he might be, and no doubt was, but he never ever lacked courage.

I found it harder to believe in the Lady Macbeth of Cheryl Campbell. Though she was very good in keeping the dinner party going when Macbeth was seeing Banquo's ghost, I thought she dithered too much in the final mad scene, scrubbed her hands too hard, whimpered too pathet-ically. Partly this had to do with the absurd metal fire-escape ladder she was required to climb to reach her bed chamber.

Parts of the production I liked, lots of it I hated. It lacked visual magic and theatricality. There was one glorious feast scene with a table blazing with candles and silver goblets and bowls of fruit, but it lasted all of twenty seconds.

For the rest of the time we had a black space with a tall door stage right set with mirrors. And what was the back-cloth of giant green celery meant to signify? I thought perhaps shortage of money required that huge stage to be bare of scenery until I read somewhere that it was covered in miles of real black silk. Did no one sit out front and realize calico would have the same effect three rows off? Oh yes, and I could have done with some music – possibly bagpipes.

# Unfinished Business

## Barbican: The Pit, 18 February 1994

In the summer months of 1940 'Operation Sealion', code name for the proposed German invasion of Britain, was rumoured to be imminent. Bombing raids were expected, followed by enemy troop landings at Lyme Regis, Brighton, Bexhill and Ramsgate. The Royal family were warned to prepare themselves for evacuation to Canada.

Michael Hastings' densely plotted new play, *Unfinished Business*, currently in repertory at the Pit, opens and closes with an old man called Beamish, parked in a wheelchair on a disused tennis court, talking about the past to his nurse. The convalescent home on the backcloth was formerly the grand country house in which he grew up and where, during that dangerous summer 50 years before, five fascists – himself when a youth, his parents Lord and Lady Sheffield, the Bishop of Devon and the lady commandant of the Liverpool police force – waited to welcome the Germans.

Young Beamish, an arrogant, selfish, idealistic lad, spends his time either on the tennis court or up in the attic seducing Feebs, the fifteen-year-old maid. She loves him and wants him to run off with her to somewhere warm like Honolulu; he hankers for the pure life of cold baths, unheated bedrooms and vegetarian meals. The household, while waiting for Adolf's army, is looked after by Douglas, the butler, once a member of the starving unemployed. Limping like Goebbels, equally articulate and servile, he is none the less accused of being a spy after being found on his hands and knees in the attic, prising up the floorboards and unearthing guns and hand-grenades. Actually, the weapons had been put there by young Beamish, who had stolen them from the weekend luggage belonging to the Bishop of Devon. Douglas, waving a gun, every inch the servant and anxious to please, finally pretends he has denounced the family to the Home Guard and the police. Lord Sheffield grapples with him, the gun goes off and Douglas drops dead. Sheffield would have us believe that his subsequent rushing up to the attic to commit suicide is down to remorse: personally, I think he knew the Germans weren't coming after all.

Feebs, now pregnant, is dismissed. Unable to support herself, the baby is taken away from her. Some years later the child finds its mother, becomes a state registered nurse and ends up unwittingly pushing her immobilized Papa up and down the tennis court.

The smallness of the Pit stage and the closeness of the actors to the audience doesn't do justice to this provoking and emotional play. Even that marvellous actor Philip Voss seemed uneasy when he stood on the attic table with the noose about his neck. Also there's a bit too much explaining going on. We shouldn't need be told that which we've just seen. The ending, too, is not quite right. Feebs should perhaps have taken a tennis ball, as well as the hand-grenade, from her handbag. Transfixed by the sight of the latter object, Beamish wouldn't make any attempt to catch the ball she flings him. On a larger stage we could have watched it as it bounced towards the footlights, and only when it stopped should she remove the pin from the grenade and lob it towards his outstretched hands. The loud bang from the tennis court would then have been followed by an even louder gasp from the audience.

# The Government Inspector

## Tricycle Theatre, 4 March 1994

Nikolai Gogol's dramatic masterpiece, *The Government Inspector*, a satire dealing with corruption in a small provincial town far from Moscow, was first staged in 1836. Viciously attacked by the critics – though apparently the Tsar found it amusing – its author fled Russia for 12 years and only came back to die. The play, ingeniously adapted by Marie Jones for the Dubbel-joint Production Company, is now on show at the Tricycle Theatre. Having neither seen nor read the original version I have no idea whether the eating of steak featured so prominently, but it seems to me that the transplantation of the ignorant officials – Charity Commissioner, Headmaster, Judge and Mayor – from Mother Russia at the beginning of the 19th century to the province of Ulster at its close, works perfectly.

It's a wonderfully crafted play – an impoverished English gentleman, about to be slung out of the local inn for nonpayment of his bill, is mistaken for a government inspector rumoured to have arrived in the sparsely-populated town. The local officials, who for years have been evicting the peasants and shipping them off to America, close ranks and prepare to bribe their way out of trouble.

All the parts are equally meaty and essential to the action. I particularly liked the skinny little Judge of Birdy Sweeney and Niamh Linehan as the Mayor's daughters.

Whether or not Gogol would be pleased at seeing his satirical comedy turned into outright farce is another matter. He was, after all, attacking corruption and ignorance. The officials he held up to scrutiny dealt in starvation and deportation and were hardly lovable. And farce, if it is to be successful, must be played for real. The absurdity of the plot must surface slowly and build with such precision that the audience collapses from something tickled within themselves, something triggered by, yet eventually independent of, the actors.

I could have done without the sexual gestures. I know there's all those codpieces in Shakespeare, and that in Restoration comedy women's bosoms hang out and the dialogue is awash with sexual innuendo, but I don't remember actual clutching of private parts. The scene in which the Englishman is caught in bed with the Mayor's wife goes on too long. His gasps and groans to the accompaniment of the heaving coverlet are far from subtle.

The company played for all they were worth, but the audience didn't laugh as much as they should have done. I think it's because we saw they were trying too hard and didn't trust us to see the joke. When they do, they'll undoubtedly have a success on their hands.

# Me and Mamie O'Rourke

## Strand Theatre, 1 April 1994

*Me and Mamie O'Rourke* – a drama written by the American author Mary Agnes Donoghue – is in production at the
Strand Theatre, London. Though I saw it ten days ago I'm
writing this review only an hour after returning from
darkest Norfolk and a weekend attendance at the King's
Lynn Literary Festival sponsored by MacClennans Whisky.

Let me say at once that far from the demon drink wiping
out received impressions, my understanding of the play has
been sharpened, in that much of the discussion in King's
Lynn about the so-called decline of the novel, the debase-
ment of language and the deterioration in educational
standards, centred on the 'pernicious' influence of television.

The oldies amongst us, reared on a diet of *Just William*
stories, *Stalky and Co*, *Red Letter* magazine, Joseph Conrad,
Grimms' Fairy Tales, the *Jungle Book of Medicine* and those
*Saturday Night Theatre* wireless adaptations of the miracu-
lous novels of Ivy Compton Burnett, felt that on the whole
the box had done more harm than good.

We were wrong; but for television, audiences would not
be flocking to the Strand Theatre to see *Me and Mamie
O'Rourke* in which the two main characters – the one a wife
whose husband is bringing their house down about her ears,
the other a woman who walks on quicksand – are portrayed
by the TV 'stars', Jennifer Saunders and Dawn French. Not
to see it would be a pity, for this outstanding play, being at
heart a tragedy, is enacted with comic genius.

Louise (the emaciated Miss Saunders) and Bibi (the
bonny Miss French) are best friends. They support each
other through the bad times. Bibi, teetering on high heels

and even higher expectations, is forever waiting for a telephone call from the Mr Right of the previous night. Louise, bleached by cement dust and deadened by demolition noises, is waiting for her mock-Adams fireplace to fall into the basement. She is fortified by fantasies, replacing David, her unsatisfactory and mallet-wielding husband, with visions of Clark, the demon lover.

The first half of the play, which contains the much commented-on scene in which the two women wonder if it might be more beneficial to become lesbians, is achingly funny. The dramatic timing of both French and Saunders is faultless. The second half, in which the fireplace falls in pieces through the rafters and the telephone rings with the wrong message, is too near the bone for comfort. Stung by pain, the girls put into words the home truths they have kept unsaid. Louise says Bibi has always flaunted herself as a lamb ripe for slaughter; Bibi says it was Louise who provided David with his mallet. The pauses, after each confrontation, are fantastic, and the outcome – that they can never have the same relationship again – wholly convincing.

I never saw J. B. Priestley's *Johnson Over Jordan*, but I remember reading a reminiscence by the great Harold Hobson, in which he wrote that the sight of Johnson – played by the equally late and great Ralph Richardson – wearing a bowler hat, carrying a briefcase and standing at the moment of curtain-fall in the centre of an empty stage, moved him to tears. I don't think it's going overboard to equate this theatrical exit with Miss French's departure into a frightening future, chin gamely up, suitcase in hot little hand.

What a night out, and how rare it is that play, direction (Robert Allan Ackerman), sets (Ultz) and entire cast blend into one lovely work of dramatic excellence.

# *King Lear*

## Cochrane Theatre, 15 April 1994

Much has been written on *King Lear*, from the declarations of the scholarly Dr Johnson to the informed criticism of Harold Hobson. Reviewing a production directed by and starring Olivier in 1946, Hobson, after lamenting the removal of the Old Vic from its bombed-out premises in the Waterloo Road to the New Theatre in the West End (stall seats extravagantly priced at 13/6) wrote:

> Under one aspect this play presents man as the plaything of the gods; they kill us for their sport. Where the quarry is lame or feeble or impotent, surely the sport is poor? It was said of the Duke of Marlborough that he could be bought, but that he was worth buying. Mr Olivier's Lear is a man who by temperament is capable of being tortured, but he is worth torturing.

Two hundred years earlier, Dr Johnson observed, 'There is perhaps no play which keeps the attention so strongly fixed; which so much agitates our passions and interest . . . the sudden changes of fortune, and the quick succession of events, fill the mind with a perpetual tumult of indignation, pity and hope.'

The talented Talawa Company, now performing *King Lear* at the Cochrane Theatre in Southampton Row, has a comparatively young man, Ben Thomas, in the leading role – Wolfit played it at the same age – but he is very strong. The possessor of a splendid voice and a magnificent stage presence, he might have soared were it not for a production which, in its inability to know in what direction it's heading, left him no alternative but to keep his feet firmly on the ground.

Some of the dilemma, the unfortunate mingling of styles – coming up to the interval that excellent actress Mona Hammond sang 'The rain it raineth every day' to the tune of 'Raindrops keep falling on my head' – can perhaps be explained by a daft piece of psychiatric irrelevance in the programme: 'Lear is angry, confused, disturbed and mentally ill. Cordelia, married and living elsewhere, senses his isolation and returns to support him. Back to basics is captured in this play. Adultery, rivalry and the mixed feelings which children have for their parents are as powerfully represented as the possessiveness of those same parents.'

Surely the whole point of a masterpiece lies in its timelessness; it doesn't need to be brought up to date. With the exception of the much-acclaimed revival of Priestley's *An Inspector Calls*, I'm not against innovation or fresh interpretation; the thing is, there must be consistency. If Edmund, in the latter half of the drama, is going to prance about among monkishly garbed figures banging on riot shields, we can't be expected to sustain our feelings of anger against Goneril and Regan for failing their father so lamentably.

I ask you, what daughter would want, never mind have the tenancy of a property spacious enough, to take in a Dad who insisted on bringing along a retinue of 100 souls? That said, I liked David Harewood as Edmund and Cathy Tyson and Lolita Chakrabarti as the maligned sisters.

This production did fill one with a perpetual tumult of indignation, pity and hope, but not always in the right places.

# Les Misérables

## Palace Theatre, 29 April 1994

The last time I was in Paris I visited Victor Hugo's house, which is now a museum. Until then I thought he'd only written novels and was surprised to learn he was also a play-wright, though not, according to the *Oxford Companion to the Theatre*, a very good one. With the exception of *Ruy Blas*, which the critics disliked because the hero killed himself for the wrong reasons, his work apparently suffered from 'overloading, from a plethora of words and details, from too much erudition and from not enough emotion.'

Nor did I know that Hugo had been expelled from France in 1851 and gone to live first in Jersey and then Guernsey, where he wrote *Les Misérables*. His son turned the book into a play, but it's not his adaptation that is still playing to full houses at the Palace Theatre.

After seeing the production last Monday night I can well understand its enormous and continuing success – it is now playing its ninth year – for it is directed with stunning theatricality, has a dramatic storyline, wonderful sets, stirring songs, and a cast positively jumping with energy.

Mostly, *Les Misérables* is about redemption. Valjean, released from a nineteen-year prison sentence for stealing a loaf of bread, is reduced to thieving again, this time from the saintly Bishop of Digne who has taken him into his house for the night. When caught with a pair of silver candlesticks Valjean is dragged in front of the Bishop who pretends the silver was not stolen but freely given. From then on Valjean reforms and spends his life being nice to the poor.

And what poor there were in those days! Victor Hugo

wrote: 'People reduced to the extremity of need are also driven to the limits of their resources, and woe to any defenceless person who comes in their way. Work and wages, food and warmth, courage and goodwill – all is lost to them. The daylight dwindles into shadow, and the darkness enters their hearts . . . no horror is then excluded.

'Desperation is bounded only by the flimsiest of walls . . . they appear utterly depraved, vile and odious; it is rare for those who have sunk so low not to be degraded in the process, and there comes a point, moreover, where the unfortunate and infamous are grouped together, merged in a single fateful world. They are the outcasts, the underdogs, *Les Misérables.*'

No wonder there was a revolution. The most visually thrilling scene in this entirely thrilling production is of the barricades, a jagged mountain of wooden debris that climbs almost to the flies. The cannons roar, the smoke rises, the music reaches a crescendo and the urchin boy, Gavroche, clambers over the top in search of ammunition. Then everything goes quiet, the stage revolves, and you see the other side and the dead strewn like baubles on a Christmas tree.

At curtain fall the audience stood up to clap. We wouldn't let the cast go, and in the end the cast applauded us.

# Jack, A Night On The Town With John Barrymore

## Criterion Theatre, 24 June 1994

I read most of the reviews of *Jack, A Night On The Town With John Barrymore*, an entertainment devised and acted by Nicol Williamson, and almost all hinted at disappointment in the content of the piece. The general opinion seemed to be that in failing to uncover the dark forces which drove Barrymore to drunken ruin, the audience had been cheated of an insight into the nature of Mr Williamson's own particular genius.

I couldn't disagree more. At the matinée at the Criterion on Saturday, it was quite clear why Williamson has such power. For one, he's tall, has superb balance, and a pleasing, if sad, face. Also, he has a superb voice and delivery. As to why John Barrymore drank, womanized, barn-stormed his way to the grave – he was an actor for God's sake, not a bank manager, and in any case he didn't die until he was 60, a sensible age at which to kick the bucket, particularly if looks, wealth, work and wives are vanishing into the sunset.

Williamson wrote his one-man play after appearing on Broadway as Barrymore's ghost in *I Hate Hamlet*. Barrymore, brother to the equally successful thespians, Lionel and Ethel, started out in vaudeville; he could hoof and sing. Before becoming the greatest classical actor America had ever known, and then one of the first stars of its cinema, he was a matinée idol in light comedies with such memorable titles as *Captain Jinks of the Horse Marines* and *Believe Me, Xantippe*.

He earned enormous sums of money, and married once too often. One gets the impression that it wasn't his fault, failing at matrimony. He would have liked to be a family man, to be faithful, but his sex and his fame conspired against him.

Nicol Williamson, as Barrymore, rips through the scene in which Richard III woos and wins the queen whose husband he has just murdered. 'I wasn't going to play it as a cripple,' he says, 'I just turned in one foot and lifted one shoulder.' For a few seconds Barrymore muses on what made him run hell for leather towards self-destruction. It was some incident when he was fourteen – either he got into bed with his stepmother or she got into bed with him – which, when you think about it, is a bit similar to poor old Hamlet's can of worms. Personally, I think he was just too talented to be anything but solitary.

In 1925 Barrymore performed *Hamlet* at the Haymarket Theatre. One of the reviews contained this passage: 'It is an awkward thing, being in front of the footlights, to figure as a personified problem, a walking mystery. Your first need, which you must feel in your bones, is to be human, natural, comprehensible . . . one accepts the inconsistencies of character because, first of all, they are in the text; and secondly, because the actor is so manifestly sincere.' Quite so. Mr Williamson is a man of parts. He has vision, voice, grace; he is altogether that sweet, problematical prince.

# Home

## Wyndham's Theatre, 22 July 1994

I didn't see the first production of David Storey's *Home* which opened at the Royal Court 24 years ago with Gielgud and Richardson in the leading roles, although I do remember watching a television profile of Richardson in which, discussing the play, he remarked, 'Johnny and I didn't understand a word of it.' He was being ingenuous, of course, and doubtless referring to the many lines of dialogue which peter out in mid-sentence.

I always enjoy intervals, in that one can have a ciggie and listen to the comments of fellow theatregoers. Unless one is wholly confident, it helps to know what other people think. As a good half of a London audience is usually foreign, eavesdropping is not often enlightening, but at the matinée performance of *Home* at Wyndham's I did pick up a few hints. An oldish man foolishly wearing shorts declared it was all about class, and a young girl said it was boring. I thought they were both wrong, the girl spectacularly so, though I do see that a lack of experience of life, and in particular of the way life used to be, could influence her opinion. As to class, although *Home* is mostly about people's inability to communicate, in this case it can't all be put down to differences of background and education.

*Home* is about two women and two men who meet in what appears to be the grounds of some enormous hotel in the country. It's obviously summertime because Jack wears a blazer and Harry a very smart lightweight suit. The women, splendidly played by Brenda Bruce and Rowena Cooper, are ignorant, foul-mouthed and inarticulate. The men, bordering on the refined, find it equally difficult to express themselves. In spite of sharing a common language they prefer to converse in clichés; it saves time and avoids embarrassment, though the former commodity is something they have in abundance.

Jack, the more chatty of the two, talks about numerous cousins on his father's side, and Harry struggles to convey memories of the war. Off they go for a walk and on come the two 'girls', and almost immediately we realize the hotel is an enormous mental institution.

Once this becomes clear the play slumps a bit, but only in suspense. Although nothing in the way of intricacy of plot is going to happen from now on, it doesn't matter a damn. Indeed, it allows one to concentrate on the superb perform-ances given by Paul Eddington as Harry and Richard Briers as Jack.

It seems to me that both actors are equally good. Mr Eddington would appear to have the better part, in that his agony of mind is more obvious, and he's more innocent. His shyness when the women approach him, his pathetic delight at making friends, his efforts to release words from his tortuously working mouth render him pitiful. He is a man one feels sorry for right from the beginning.

Mr Briers, on the other hand, takes longer to arouse com-passion in the audience. Jack has always had to work at making people like him, and he still remembers how to go through the motions; show an interest in the other fellow's conversation; don't be boastful; be firm in your opinion and yet allow the other's point of view. He breaks down only when he can't keep up the pretence any longer that the sun is shining and all's right with the world. A lesser actor than Mr Briers would have made a meal of Jack's lapses into reality. As it is, he beautifully underplays these moments; we know he's weeping but we don't hear a sound.

If you go and see *Home*, be sure to take a handkerchief with you.

# A Busy Day

## King's Head Theatre, 5 August 1994

Fanny Burney was born in King's Lynn in 1752. Twenty-six years later she wrote a best-selling novel entitled *Evelina*, followed by a play, *The Witlings*, the latter work satirizing the intellectual literati who now lionized her. Charles Burney, her father, horrified that she should bite the hand that fed her, promptly persuaded her to become a second Keeper of the Robes to Queen Charlotte, thus sentencing her to five years of hard labour and stifling boredom.

Afterwards, she recovered sufficiently to write three more novels, none of which were liked as much as *Evelina*, and several plays which were even less successful, one of them being the comedy *A Busy Day*, now in performance at the King's Head Theatre, Islington.

The director, Alan Coveney, found the text in an academic paperback while browsing among the shelves of a remainder bookshop in Bristol. It does seem astonishing that it's never been staged until now, and even more astonishing, seeing as it's the sort of play that relies heavily on people rushing in and out of different doors, that the cramped space of the King's Head does little to diminish its cracking pace and crackling wit.

In spite of the bigotry and snobbery exhibited by the characters and the biting and clever dialogue, the piece is never really malicious. Nobody loses out; even the dreadful Sir Marmaduke gets what he wants in the end. At the time that she wrote it, Fanny had at last got away from Dad and was married to General d'Arblay, so perhaps that's why it's a happy play.

As to plot, after being rapped over the knuckles for giving

away the identity of the murderer in *The Mousetrap* the other week – I've already forgotten who he was, except that he arrived on skis – I'll be brief.

An heiress of low background loves and is loved by Cleveland, brother to Frank, nephew of Sir Marmaduke. Miss Percival loves Cleveland. Frank loves anybody who has a few bob. Nobody loves Sir Marmaduke. There's a sister to Frank and Cleveland who is lovable, and a cousin to someone or other whom the audience loved. Everybody misunderstands one another, but it all turns out well in the end.

Most of the cast did their jobs splendidly, particularly Juliette Grassby as Miss Percival, Paul Nicholson as the cousin, Brendan Hooper as Lord John Dervis and Ian Kelly as Frank. As I can't remember the name of the heiress and the cast list isn't printed in order of appearance, I can't work out who played her, but I enjoyed the actress's performance very much.

If, like me, you're interested in Dr Samuel Johnson and the age he lived in, this is a production you ought to see. Introduced to Fanny at Mrs Thrale's in Streatham, the Doctor thought her a good thing. Following the death of Mr Thrale, and his influence on the brewer's household fading, Johnson bemoaned the fact that he was no longer invited to parties. Miss Burney, in her diary of 1782, confirms he had reasons for complaint. 'He is constantly omitted,' she wrote, 'either from too much respect or too much fear.' When he lay dying she stood weeping in the doorway of his bedchamber.

There's no character in the play remotely like Dr Johnson, but the manners and attitudes of the time are very clear; in fact, nothing much seems to have changed, apart from the sorry reduction in our language. The cousin in *A Busy Day*, castigating Lady Whilhelmina for her rudeness, spouts a cascade of words. Nowadays, 'You piss me off' would suffice, which possibly explains why modern plays are so short.

# Don't Dress for Dinner

## Duchess Theatre, September 1994

Not expecting very much, I went last week to the matinée of *Don't Dress for Dinner* at the Duchess Theatre. I'd seen most other shows, and of those I hadn't, either the management wouldn't give me a press ticket or else the play would have finished its run by the time this review came out.

One should never judge a book by its cover, or, for that matter, the quality of a production by the quotes on the billboards. Nor should one ignore the explanatory notes in those programmes devoted to enlightening an audience rather than extolling the virtues of the nearest restaurant. The *Don't Dress for Dinner* programme was exemplary, and I'm happy to pass on some of its wisdom.

Marc Camoletti, author of the present play at the Duchess, also wrote that smash hit *Boeing Boeing*, both dramas being skilful examples of the type of light farce popularized in France as 'boulevard comedy'. Towards the last quarter of the 18th century, a dancer called Jean-Baptiste Nicola established a theatre south of the Boulevard Voltaire devoted to performing the great and spectacular pieces of Talconet, known affectionately as 'the Molière of the Boulevard'. (No, I'd never heard of him either.) The works of the boulevardier writers, with their contempt for moralizing and literary style, their rejection of the abstract, were designed for popular consumption. Domestic affairs turned always on love (adultery) and money. The chief characters were always the husband, the wife and a third partner, either mistress or lover.

Skip a hundred years or so, and Alfred Jarry dropped the bomb which was his *Ubu Roi*. After that, modernism entered the theatre. Audiberti, Ionesco, Beckett – authors of the so-called metaphysical farces based on the human condition stripped down to its bare, ridiculous essentials – took precedence. Thus we arrive at the present masters of the genre, like Jean Anouilh (yes, I thought he was posher) and André Roussin who wrote *The Little Hut*, in which that *Oldie* boy, David Tomlinson, shone so brightly.

It's my personal opinion, after two or so years of theatre reviewing, that either a play has to make one cry – *Street of Crocodiles, Home, Les Misérables* – gasp with fear – *The Woman in Black, The Invisible Man, Misery* – snort with rage – *An Inspector Calls* – bounce in one's seat with exuberance – *Buddy, Five Guys Named Moe, Crazy for You*, the muddy *Midsummer Night's Dream* – forget the play and remember only the actors – Peter O'Toole, Dawn French, Robert Stephens and Nicol Williamson – or else hoot with laughter – *Run for Your Wife* and *Don't Dress for Dinner*.

The latter is a wonderful, superbly structured romp. In spite of the fact that the theatre was a bit empty, I couldn't stop guffawing out loud. Royce Mills as the devious yet good-hearted husband was a joy. I think I remember him years ago in *Crossroads*, when he strayed in from *The Archers*. Possibly he was the first Nigel Pargiter, the one whose aristocratic Mummy is currently hitting the bottle and who is about to marry the naughty Elizabeth. Anyway, Mr Mills's timing is marvellous, as is that of Michael Sharvell Martin as his friend, Robert, who looks like a cross between Michael Gambon and that dear dead chap, Nigel Stock, who used to play Dr Watson.

I'm beginning to think, with the exception of good old Will Shakespeare and the Time plays of J. B. Priestley, that farce is the bestest, cleverest, subtlest form of theatre to be seen today.

# 1995

Death of Peter Cook, Ginger Rogers, Eva Gabor, Stephen Spender, Ida Lupino, Dean Martin and the gangster, Ronnie Kray.

Diana, Princess of Wales, opens her heart on television and talks for the first time about Charles and Camilla. 'I loved my husband, but there were three of us in the marriage.'

*Dangerous Corner* by J. B. Priestley is about a group of people who, starting an evening together as friends, end up exposed as nothing of the sort. Adultery, homosexuality and betrayal rear up after the pudding is served.

# Oliver!

## London Palladium, January 1995

Although the book of Lionel Bart's musical adaptation of Charles Dickens's *Oliver Twist* is, by necessity, not half as dense as the original, I think Dickens would be pleased with this new production at the London Palladium. He'd enjoy the catchy tunes and the theatrical magic of the sets, and would – if we can take the word of his biographer and friend John Forster that he wasn't a conceited man – no doubt congratulate Mr Bart for making an engaging and joyous romp out of a dark and sentimental story.

Dickens had such prodigious creative energy – between 1837 and '38 he was engaged not only on *Oliver Twist* but also *The Pickwick Papers*, *Nicholas Nickleby* and the editing of a *Life of Grimaldi* – that I imagine he wouldn't have minded what anybody did with anything he wrote.

He sent a letter the following year to the actor Macready, who had obviously put on something written by Dickens, full of commiseration for the failure of the piece and assurances that it was he (Dickens) who was at fault rather than the production.

It's true that the orphanage in which little Ollie was systematically starved wasn't a figment of Dicken's imagination, any more than were the likes of Fagin or Bill Sykes, but then, times change and we must all move on.

It's interesting that a recent episode of *Brookside* featured four children on the Close being picked up for shoplifting. They were into nicking Game Boys and videos rather than handkerchiefs, but the crime was the same, that of thieving, and none of them are likely to be deported or sent to jail. Nor did they, though all have perfectly dreadful parents, break out into Oliver's tear-jerking refrain of 'Where is Love?'. Little Leo from the Pizza takeaway, whose Dad is about to be taken away for armed robbery, snivelled with genuine contrition, and Rachel told her Mum she was sorry and swore she would never do it again, but by then the police were digging up the patio under which her Dad is mouldering. Perhaps Mr Bart should do a musical about *Brookside*.

I thought this new production of *Oliver!* directed by Sam Mendes was very good, if not at all frightening. Jonathan Pryce's politically-correct Fagin was more like Peter Pan than Shylock, and James Daley in the title role made one believe that good breeding will always triumph in the end. Sally Dexter as Nancy was terrific – neither of my grandchildren caught on that she was on the game – and so was Miles Anderson in the role of Bill Sykes. Now, he was frightening, stout as his bulldog and equally incapable of control once his dander was up. Of course, his sort still exist, though nowadays we've been 'educated' to believe that such potential brutality can be eliminated by loving parenting. What nobody's told us is what constitutes love.

# New England

## Barbican: The Pit, February 1995

*New England*, by the American Richard Nelson, performed by the RSC and now in repertory at the Pit in the Barbican, is a very good play. All the characters, save for Alice – a tremendous performance by Angela Thorne – are English and all, for one reason or another have come to live and work in the States. The men, in particular, are continually mocking the manners and language of their adopted country.

They're not the first to do so, and there are some splendid quotes in the programme to do with other people's reactions. 'The thing that impresses me most is the way parents obey their children.' (Edward VIII) 'If I had a definition of capitalism I would say the process whereby American girls turn into American women.' (Christopher Hampton) 'Contrary to popular belief, English women do not wear tweed nightgowns.' (Hermione Gingold)

None of the characters in the play have 'ordinary' jobs; they're script-readers for film companies, professors of music, voice coaches for the theatre or something in publishing. The exception is Alice, who's just a woman. The action takes place over two days in a farmhouse in Western Connecticut, home of Harry and Alice.

Most of the structure of the piece hangs on Tom, beautifully played by Mick Ford, a dialect coach for off-Broadway theatre and still very English, who has been invited for the weekend by Alice because she'd recently bumped into him in New York and he once used to be her brother-in-law. Tom arrives, greets his morose host, mutters a few politenesses, scuttles out of the room to collect his overnight bag and hears a shot fired. Harry has committed suicide.

Not having expected quite such a fun weekend, Tom wants to leave but feels it would be like deserting a sinking ship. Harry's family are sent for, twin brother Alfred, two daughters, a son and a bitch of a daughter-in-law.

If this was an early Arthur Miller play we would be in for a depressing night of dark secrets and home truths. In fact, there's plenty of both in *New England*, but I found the play immensely funny. Other people were laughing too.

The cast is so strong and the parts so well written that one keeps changing one's opinion of the characters. Elizabeth (Selina Cadell) who at first seems bossy and insensitive, turns out to be the most emotional; Annie Corbier as Sophie, dreadful wife to Duncan Bell's wet husband, is more sinned against than sinning; and the arty-farty Gemma ends up being the nicest to poor insulted Tom. David Burke as Alfred is a joy to watch and a fit partner for Angela Thorne's Alice, a woman whom life has tossed about and whose voice gloriously resembles that of the late Katharine Hepburn.

I suppose one could say the play is about rootlessness and people being restless, and Mr Nelson does have an affinity with Chekhov, but for me, coming so soon after Christmas, it reminded me of how important it is for families to get together and put the boot in. Better to remember how you parted than not to remember you met. This production, acting, writing and direction perfectly blended, makes a night at the theatre an enchantment.

# Three Tall Women
## Wyndham's Theatre

# Dangerous Corner
## Whitehall
## March 1995

I've been to see two plays in the last month, Edward Albee's *Three Tall Women* at Wyndham's Theatre and J. B. Priestley's *Dangerous Corner* at the Whitehall. The former show is notable for the outstanding performances of Maggie Smith and Frances de la Tour, the latter for a construction of plot which is well-nigh perfect.

Albee, asked what gave him the idea for his play, brought up an image of his infant self in his Nanny's arms on a grassy knoll watching a house being built, flanked by his adoptive mother and father. He said: 'I knew I did not want to write a revenge piece – could not honestly do so, for I felt no need for revenge. We [his adoptive mother and he] had managed to make each other very unhappy over the years, but I was past all that. Though it is true I did not like her much, could not abide her prejudices, her loathings, her paranoias, I admired her pride, her sense of self.'

The things we hate in those closest to us are not often perceived by other people. The character played by Maggie Smith, bigoted, incontinent and old as hell, was loved by the audience at Wyndham's; one or two of us would have swopped our own more acceptable mothers for the gloriously arrogant and dotty old biddy twitching and snarling centre stage.

Of course, being rich she could afford to be nasty to those attending to her, and having lived an obviously full life her ramblings were considerably more riveting than those of your average OAP closeted in a council flat. What she was rambling on about was her son – no good – her husband – too small – and horses. She was also raging against having had to come to terms with who she was.

In the second half the impressively elegant Frances de la Tour showed us who she was in middle years, and Anastasia Hille played her when young. This multiplicity of selves was a shade confusing, and I'm not sure the second act worked all that well.

I felt I'd been led to expect an ending of real profundity, something that would redeem the wicked old witch, and it didn't happen. Not that it mattered. The first act was sheer magic. Maggie Smith was so old as to be no longer female. Every gesture, rasp of the voice, working of the mouth was an impersonation of a pantomime dame, and yet the character was real and horribly recognizable.

On the other hand, with the exception of Christopher Timothy as Stanton and Keith Baxter as Robert Caplan, the characters in Priestley's *Dangerous Corner* weren't real at all, at least as played by the cast at the Whitehall Theatre. It was a pity because the plot is marvellous.

A group of friends gather at a dinner party. They know each other well and are apparently at ease with one another. Then, in the course of the evening, the cracks begin to show, until by the end each one is exposed as something quite different.

I believed in Keith Baxter, though he has a funny walk. He played his part with passion, and his final speech in the last act, when he realizes he's lived among illusions, was well done and moving.

OK, the play is a bit dated. Adultery and insider dealing and homosexuality hardly raise eyebrows anymore. But my word, Priestley can't half tell a story.

# My Night with Reg

## Criterion Theatre, May 1995

*My Night with Reg* at the Criterion isn't for the shy at heart. It might be best to go alone, wearing dark glasses, and to have had the benefit of a bohemian upbringing. The lady in the seat next to me wore shades and she was quite composed throughout. Mind you, her spectacles were extremely dark and she was helped up the aisle when it was over, so possibly she was visually challenged.

The play, by Kevin Elyot, is billed as a comedy, though there are two funerals in it, one for Reg who never appears and the other for poor, lonely Guy, both of whom have obviously succumbed to AIDS. All the characters, save for Benny the bus driver – his trousers are too tight – and Eric the decorator, weep at one point or another. And yet it is a very funny play, which is not to say it's a comedy. I suppose I wanted to see a lot of camping it up, all harmless innuendo rather than a blatant spelling out of the love that dare not speak its name. It's very savage.

There are six in the cast, and it's impossible to praise one actor above another. They're so excellent it's a pity they have to take off their drawers, which I found disconcerting rather than interesting. I kept wondering how my Dad, he who once stormed out of the Palace cinema in Southport because Claude Raines was too convincing a libertine, would have survived such an onslaught of full frontals.

The plot is simple. Reg, Daniel's lover, dies, and Guy holds a wake. Daniel hopes he was the only one Reg cleaved to, though why he should think that, seeing they're all rutting like stags, God knows. John has had a proper affair – meaning he loved him – with Reg. Guy loves John, unrequitedly. Benny has had it off with Reg, as have Guy, Eric and Bernie.

Every time John Sessions as Daniel comes on stage the whole thing lights up, which is unfair because everyone else is equally splendid, whether it be David Bamber as the vulnerable Guy, Roger Frost as the boringly nice Bernie, Kenneth MacDonald as deplorable Benny or Anthony Calf as John, the golden boy. Had the play gone on longer I think John would have died next; he was looking much paler by the end. As for Joe Duttine as Eric, he gives a lovely, believable performance as a nice normal boy who regards the other five with humour and compassion.

The dawn chorus began on the soundtrack soon after he and John had been to bed – nothing rude took place because John was still pining for the dead Reg – but I didn't hear the birds until the two chaps had mercifully covered up their parts. Then Daniel, alias John Sessions, arrived, clothes soiled with mud and semen after a night spent cavorting in the undergrowth of Hampstead Heath. Maybe Sessions shouts louder than anyone else, or perhaps he has that explosive quality which makes one fear something dreadful is going to happen whenever he appears. Whatever it is, he dominates the stage.

# Absolute Hell

## National Theatre, July 1995

Much of *Absolute Hell*, the absolutely fabulous play now showing at the National Theatre, will be lost on those still in the bloom of youth, seeing that in the past the sort of behaviour exhibited by the characters was almost always accompanied by a sense of guilt, something which seems to have vanished along with so much else. Without an understanding of the background – the ending of the war, the lurch towards socialism, a belief in the coming of Utopia – the play could be mistaken for a rip-roaring comedy. Still, I suppose the same could be said of most plays, including *King Lear*.

*Absolute Hell* was written by Rodney Ackland. Born in 1908, he studied at the Central School of Speech Training and Dramatic Art and later wrote over 30 theatre and half a dozen screen plays, among the latter an adaptation of A. J. Cronin's novel, *Hatter's Castle*. I saw this particular film in adolescence, and though I can't remember the plot I do recall thinking its portrayal of family life bore a remarkable resemblance to my own, give or take a few butlers.

Ackland's play, *Birthday*, shown in 1934, explored the same sort of middle class set-up as Dodie Smith's hugely popular drama, *Dear Octopus*. Trouble was, Ackland's piece was penned with the ferocity of a Wycherley and closed after a week.

The Pink Room, the original title of *Absolute Hell*, rejected by H. M. Tennant as ugly and distasteful, was rescued by Terence Rattigan who backed its 1952 production. To a man, the critics savaged it, not least Harold Hobson, a response scarcely credible to a modern audience well used to introspection.

Ackland never recovered from this reception, though it's comforting to know that at least his personal life picked up. Queer to start with, or possibly always bisexual, in his forties he fell in love with and married Mab, daughter of Frederick Lonsdale. It was true love and he had a breakdown when she died of cancer.

*Absolute Hell* is set in a club in Soho, a mixture of the French Pub and the Colony Rooms, at the end of the war. The members drink a lot and some of them have a touching belief in Art. Every now and then a character based on the late Robert Newton falls though the doors and is heaved out. A lady tramp called Madge climbs though the window and hands out leaflets to do with the sayings of the Virgin Mary.

For those unbelievers out there who think Ackland had a vivid imagination, please read Alan Bennett's book about Miss Shepherd, she who took up residence in a urine-sodden van in his front yard in Camden Town. The actress Alison Fisk plays Madge and is utterly believable.

Judi Dench as Christine, manager of the club, is the star of the show. Being a superlative actress Miss Dench plays it for real, waddles with buttocks thrust out, flings her throaty voice up to the Gods. It's a marvellous performance, a unique blending of technical excellence and imaginative power. The first act ends with her being stripped to her corsets by passing GIs. Terrified at being left alone, her squeals of welcome at their drunken attentions are shocking.

At first, Greg Hicks, in the role of the young Ackland, sank below my expectations, if only because I'd watched Bill Nighy in the television production. I thought Hicks was copying him too much, and then, after a bit, I gave in. Hicks plays the writer whose career has been early blighted by a crushing review and whose weakness of character has turned him into a drunk and a tart. His despair is often comic, which is at it should be, and Hicks, against all the odds, manages to make him appear courageous rather than pitiable. However, he's not always audible; not everyone sits in the first three rows of the stalls.

There are over 30 actors in the cast and all of them – including Alan Cox, Helen Fraser, Betty Marsden and Peter Woodthorpe (he who portrays the maliciously camp film producer) – play their parts to perfection. Get the right director, in this case Anthony Page, and British theatre is second to none. Get the right play and the sky's the limit.

Betjeman wrote a poem in 1954 which sums up this particular drama, the last verse of which reads:

There was sun enough for lazing upon beaches,
There was fun enough far into the night,
But I'm dying now and done for,
What on earth was all that fun for?
For I'm old and ill and terrified and tight.

# Hot Mikado

## Queen's Theatre, August 1995

It was the tumbling down of a Japanese sword from a wall in the house of W. S. Gilbert that inspired the writing of The Mikado. First produced in 1885 at the Savoy Theatre, the then Japanese ambassador tried to have it suppressed. He said it was disrespectful to the Emperor. It was a tremendous success, although Queen Victoria thought it rather silly. I saw it once in an amateur production and was bewildered by chaps and maidens in oriental costumes singing music-hall songs.

In 1938 two separate adaptations, *Swing Mikado* and *Hot Mikado*, appeared on Broadway, the latter backed by Mike Todd – one of Elizabeth Taylor's many husbands – with a cast of 150 black Americans headed by that superb tap-dancer Bill (Bojangles) Robinson.

I've been reading up on what the experts think of Black Musicals and by and large the received opinion is that they're at best patronizing and at worst degrading. There was a show put on in 1898 called *A Trip to Coontown*, and in 1928 the celebrated Florence Mills sang 'I'm a Little Black-bird Looking for a Bluebird'. Although Bojangles later starred in Shirley Temple movies, his career was strictly limited by the attitudes expected of a man with a dark skin; he had to be an exuberant Uncle Tom. Most of the black musicals, even *Porgy and Bess*, were meant for white audiences.

The present production of *Hot Mikado*, now showing at the Queen's Theatre, doesn't rely on the 1938 show. None of the original material could be found and David H. Bell and Rob Bowman have devised their own version. Judging by the standing ovation on the first night and the fact that it's still running, they've done so very successfully.

For myself, I was baffled by the concept of Japanese courtiers in modern dress going along with ideas of life and death that existed a century ago. Also, and with the best will in the world – possibly to do with old newsreels – I've always thought of the Japanese as being very decorous, bowing at the drop of a hat and always taking their shoes off. I didn't expect them to be shaking their hips and hot-shoe-shuffling with the best of them. Also, the noise was tremendous.

That said, Ross Lehman as Ko-Ko was extremely good, as was Richard Lloyd King as Pooh-Bah and Paul Maunel as Nanki Poo. When Lawrence Hamilton as the Mikado strode on and began his tap-dance routine, my heart lifted. Sadly, it didn't stay up for very long, and though most of the cast had steel tips to their shoes they didn't do more than execute a token three beat bang-bang-shuffle. Why, oh why, have musicals abandoned real dancing in favour of gestures?

I expect the show will run for a very long time – it certainly has the energy – but then one man's meat, etc. I'm afraid I'm with Queen Victoria on this one.

# Communicating Doors

## Gielgud Theatre, September 1995

It strikes me as relevant, in reviewing *Communicating Doors*, Alan Ayckbourn's latest drama now showing at the Gielgud Theatre, to quote from J. B. Priestley's preface to the 1937 edition of *Time and the Conways* and *I Have Been Here Before*. In it, the great man wrote that although inspired by the theories of J. W. Dunne (the Stephen Hawking of his day) he chose to leave off where Dunne began: 'All I suggest is that the single and Universal Time that is imagined to be hastening everything to decay and dissolution is an illusion, that our real selves are the whole stretches of our lives, and that at any given moment during these lives, we are merely taking a three-dimensional cross-section of a four, or multidimensional reality.'

Always supposing you're still with me, only the other night the World Service broadcast an item on some scientist who at this moment is grappling with the very same dimensional theory. No less a person than Patrick Moore gave his opinion that the possibility of time travel is no more absurd than the probability of moon landings to an earlier generation.

Time, and not for the first time, is what Ayckbourn is on about in *Communicating Doors*. Reece, an old man at the beginning of the play, has put on paper his involvement in the murder of his two wives, one thrown out of a window, the other drowned. A call girl is summoned to sign his confession in the suite of a rather grand hotel. Baldly put, not to say confusingly, the hired tart spins into past and present through a cupboard connected to the adjoining room inhabited by Ruella, Reece's first wife. Ruella, who is not yet dead, sets about altering the future for herself and Jessica the second wife. There's also a comic security guard and a sinister solicitor.

This intriguing and ultimately flawed piece lacks structure, the revolving cupboard rapidly becoming on a par with the obligatory doors in a bedroom farce. Nor did I really believe in the character of Ruella. She looks capable, down to earth and wholly sensible. Her voice is moderate, her hairstyle fashionable, her dressing gown suitably modern, and yet she takes on board, without soulsearching, shock or any reference to her own particular history, the notion that to flit between past and presence is not all that peculiar. Worse, it is dialogue, rather than the action of the play, which explains to the audience what has happened and is going to happen.

It seems to me that Time is too profound a subject to be the stuff of comedy; we'd all like a second chance. Also, I thought that if you interfered with any given event the whole of history gets mucked up; at least that's what Captain Kirk always said in *Star Trek*, and he should know.

Priestley wrote that in the theatre 'ideas merely play like summer lightning over a deep lake of feeling . . . what is more important is that the imagination of the spectator begins to be haunted, so that long after he has left the playhouse the actors are still with him, still telling him of their despair and their hope.' I think that's what's wrong with the play – it lacks despair.

# Taking Sides

## Criterion Theatre, October 1995

I arrived for a matinée of *Taking Sides* at the Criterion Theatre, Piccadilly, in the middle of a flash flood of rain. I had an umbrella, but it buckled under the onslaught. I was 20 minutes early and was made to wait, in the company of other huddled drowned rats, in the small foyer at street level. Eventually we were let in, and down, to the bar beneath where there were four chairs. I paid one pound for a cup of coffee, 80p for a bag of crisps and was told I couldn't smoke. A gentleman next to me, shaken by the lack of comfort, ordered a double brandy. 'With ice?' asked the child behind the counter. 'Great God, no!' he answered, visibly ageing.

Climbing upwards, I came to another bar with two ashtrays and five chairs. I secured one of each, but soon gave up both owing to the number of elderly and disabled persons lounging pitifully against walls, fags held in trembling hands.

The Criterion, with its intimate auditorium, stained glass windows and tiled passages, is a beautiful theatre. Who in hell is in charge of running it? Why is it staffed with youngsters who have no inkling of the rudiments of courtesy? Surely somebody who is paid a salary for front of house management ought to round them up and tell them how to behave, and somebody even higher up ought to get off their backsides and realize that a theatre is nothing without an audience?

Having got that off my chest I count Ronald Harwood's play, *Taking Sides*, to be the best drama I've seen this year. Set in Berlin in 1946, it deals with the pre-trial interroga-

tion of the great musician, Wilhelm Furtwengler, conducted by an American army Major employed to ferret out
Nazi sympathizers. The Major is a bigoted, self-confessed
philistine, deaf to music and haunted by nightmare remem-
brances of Auschwitz. 'My eyes have seen things,' he keeps
saying, savagely swiping the needle of the gramophone
across a recording of Beethoven's Fifth Symphony.

I hated the swaggering Major; I wanted to smash his face
in when he bullied and humiliated Furtwengler. I didn't feel
that such an Aryan asshole could possibly care so much
about the Jews. I loathed him right up until the last five
minutes of the play, believing in the argument put forward
by Furtwengler – that he loved his country and felt it was
his duty, however much he hated the regime, to stay at his
post and provide his fellow citizens with the spiritual solace
of music – and then suddenly I saw what Harwood, and
Pinter, who directs, had been up to all along, and then I
swung the other way.

It's a superbly crafted play, and Daniel Massey as Furtwengler, with his discontented face and awkward walk, his
sudden glowering glances and moments of utter stillness,
gives a towering performance, but then so does Michael
Pennington as the detestable Major. The supporting cast
are equally faultless and the set is perfect. All in all, this is a
rare theatrical achievement and one which should win
every award in the book.

# Hobson's Choice
## Lyric Theatre

# *King Lear*
## Hackney Empire
## December 1995

On Wednesdays, in the small hours, I often do a spot of dusting and furniture arranging while watching the telly. Last week was no exception and at four o'clock in the morning what should be on the box but *Hobson's Choice* starring Charles Laughton and John Mills, with that marvellous sequence of the drunken Hobson seeing the moon reflected in puddles. The following afternoon I went off to the Lyric Theatre to view Frank Hauser's production of the very same play, this time with Leo McKern and Nicola McAuliffe in the leading roles.

The play stands up very well indeed and is not at all quaint, which says something for a comedy which revolves round the domination of women and class divisions prevalent at the turn of the century. Hobson, a bit of a bully but no fool, exploits Willie Mossop – the master shoemaker in his employ – and rules his household of three daughters with a rod of iron. The elder daughter revolts, marries Willie, sets up in business and brings Hobson to heel.

Though the Lancashire accents of the cast are more convincing than in the film, the characters, with the exception of Hobson and Maggie, aren't quite as real. I suppose that's inevitable when one considers how times have changed. For instance, there was something very moving about John Mills getting into his nightshirt on his wedding night, while in the play it's merely ooh la la. And when Maggie reminds

Hobson that if he doesn't settle out of court for his drunken trespass of brewery premises he'll be in the newspapers, Willie had to over-emphasize the name Manchester Guardian for fear the audience no longer remembered its importance.

That apart, the cast perform well, and in the squiffy scenes Leo McKern outclasses Laughton. There's also a wonderful and utterly believable cameo performance from Margaretta Scott as Mrs Hepworth.

Saturday night I went to see Warren Mitchell in *King Lear* at the Hackney Empire, another piece, as you know, about an exploitative old man who bullies three daughters. This very spirited production by Jude Kelly doesn't always come off, but the play itself is so magnificent it hardly matters; we still cringe beneath the onslaught of gods who in their sport tear men limb from limb like 'flies to wanton boys'. Surprisingly, I didn't object to the confusion of modern and traditional costumes, nor to the use by Tony Jones' excellent Fool of a transistor radio; the special effects, the fires, the rain, the battle, were terrific.

As for Lear, Mr Mitchell was by turns pathetic and monumental. One did see how arrogant he was, and how huge his remorse. The heath scene, in which at the height of his demented passion he commands the all-shaking thunder to 'strike flat the thick rotundity o' the world', was accompanied by such a bolt of sound as to reduce the Hackney Empire to rubble. Some people thought it drowned out his words too much, but I disagree. He was meant to shout against the elements. Consider his words at the close of the play when he enters with the hanged Cordelia:

Howl, howl, howl, howl – O! you are men of stones,
Had I your tongues and eyes, I'd use them so
That heaven's vault should crack.

# 1996

Death of Gene Kelly, Greer Garson, Beryl Reid, Michael Bentine, Willie Rushton, Ella Fitzgerald and François Mitterrand.

The end of February brings the announcement of the divorce of Diana and Prince Charles.

The Duke and Duchess of York also finalize their divorce. Fergie will make a start on her 'search for inner peace'.

*Romeo and Juliet* is a play about a man who is involved with someone else but marries a girl called Juliet. She has to pretend to be dead to avoid being bigamously wed to another man. Romeo thinks she is dead and kills himself. She wakes up, sees his body, and commits suicide. A case of marry in haste and repent at leisure.

# When The Lights Go On Again

## Conway Hall, January 1996

Only last weekend I was privileged to hear a searching discussion on the contemporary theatre which took place between the playwright, Tom Kempinski, and the Hollywood film star, David Tomlinson. Mr Kempinski, describing the finale of the first act of a new play he has written, drew a moving picture of the female heroine biting the balls off her male captive. Mr Tomlinson, well used on screen to going down in submarines, escaping from prison camps, being marooned on desert islands and baling out of blazing Spitfires, shook his head sorrowfully.

'It's done very tastefully,' Kempinski assured him. 'She does it with her back to the audience and you only see a little trickle of blood from the corner of her mouth when she turns round.'

'No, darling,' said Tomlinson firmly. 'It's quite unnecessary. She should see to his balls offstage.'

I was hoping I might review the play but unfortunately it's not yet in production, so instead went to see a slightly less controversial piece entitled *When The Lights Go On Again*, a musical entertainment based on memories of the end of World War II and excellently performed by the Age Exchange Theatre Company in celebration of the 50th anniversary of the 1945 Labour Government. The venue was the Conway Hall, Red Lion Square, and was followed by a reception hosted by Frank Dobson and Glenda Jackson.

The theatre company, a professional one, has been going for 12 years and relies heavily on nostalgia, which is no bad thing. The cast of thousands was enacted by Lynn Gardner,

Clare Summerskill and Philip Curtis. They all have fine singing voices, particularly Mr Curtis, and between them they play the banjo, the piano and something else.

I imagine the play was put on to draw our attention to the fact that we may very soon have a Labour government, even if it's not one that some oldies will easily recognize. The plot wanders from wartime Britain, in which women found certain emancipation and men faced certain death and foreign travel, to the peace years and prefabs with installed cookers and built-in wardrobes.

I did get a bit impatient with the wife who was given a flat in an old high-ceilinged house and who never stopped complaining about the space and the acres of scuffed polished floors she hadn't the money to obliterate with wall-to-wall carpeting, but that's possibly because I'm still traumatized by the sunburst floor covering I trod on as a child. Also, when they sang the old songs, we should have been told to join in. I did, lustily, but my companion thumped me into silence.

The potential power of the production, the invention, the passion of the performers, followed the example, if not the superlative expression, of the Theatre de Complicité. Long live commitment. The production coincided with a book of reflections on the election of '45, published by the Fabian Society (Bellow Publishing), edited by Austin Mitchell and with a foreword by Tony Blair. Mr Blair writes, 'A party that lives by the past is doomed to die.' He's absolutely right, but just think of the Catholic Church, or any other, for that matter. It's all a question of balls and turning one's back.

# The Glass Menagerie

## Comedy Theatre, February 1996

The other week, walking with my grandson Charlie to the Comedy Theatre to see a matinée performance of Tennessee Williams's *The Glass Menagerie*, we went through Golden Square and passed the windows of a café called Cyberspy. Charlie was through the door like a rabbit down a hole. Here one could have a snack and a half hour 'go' on the Internet for less than a fiver. While I devoured my excellent sausage sandwich he was busily Sweeping Cyberspace and Surfing the Net, terms which I gather are perfectly comprehensible to anyone between the ages of five and twenty-five. He explained to me that if he got tired of searching for the latest information on Black Holes, for instance, he could always start up a conversation with strangers living anywhere from Hong Kong to Huddersfield. It's a kind of Lonely Hearts Service on a screen. According to Charlie the standard of communication is fairly limited – 'I've a Big One' being a pretty standard character description.

*The Glass Menagerie*, the most autobiographical of Williams's plays, is about lonely people. Years ago I'd seen the great Helen Hayes in the role of the mother and I rather feared this production would not live up to the memory. I also wondered whether something I thought profound when young might now seem obvious. I needn't have worried.

The set, an apartment in a tenement building, with its fire escapes on all sides of the stage and catwalk extending right round the front of the stalls, is spectacular and marvellously lit. It's as if Laura, the daughter crippled both physically and emotionally, and her mother are trapped within a wrecked ship in a dry dock. Only the son, Tom, played by Ben Walden, ever climbs onto the surface and then only to go off to work or to the movies. Like his absconded father, he's about to run for his life.

Mother, wonderfully portrayed by Zoë Wanamaker, lives in a past filled with gentleman callers. She nags Tom into bringing home a friend from work to meet the painfully shy Laura. The first act is preparation for this momentous event, the second its inevitable outcome. In one sense, nothing much happens, at least nothing hopeful. The gentleman caller, played by Mark Dexter, is a nice boy; he's kind and encouraging to Laura and briefly she blossoms. There is a moment, when they both sit cross-legged in the candlelight and he kisses her, when one thought her Prince had come after all. Then he tells her he has to leave early to meet the girl he's going to marry.

I liked Claire Skinner as Laura. She didn't strain for the accent and was touching without being pathetic. Mark Dexter and Ben Walden were equally good, though I did get a bit tired of the device that had the latter, a sort of chorus to the action, walking endlessly round the stalls and up and down those fire escapes. Well, not tired, more anxious that he might stumble. You can give yourself a nasty knock on wrought iron.

The play, however, belongs to Zoë Wanamaker. She gives an utterly convincing performance as a woman turned monstrous by events. Miss Hayes in the role sometimes came over daft as brush. Miss Wanamaker is only too sane and infinitely more dangerous.

Afterwards I asked Charlie what he thought it had all been about. 'Families,' he said. 'Of course, they didn't have the Internet.' He didn't elaborate, but I took it that the play still worked.

# Confusions

## Richmond Theatre, March 1996

I had intended this month to review *An Old Man's Love*, a play by Michael Napier Brown based on Anthony Trollope's final novel. Those of you who've read the book will know that Mrs Bagget, housekeeper to the apparently dry old stick Whittlestaff, is one of Trollope's richest comic creations, and I was looking forward to seeing both characters brought to life on the stage of the Theatre Royal, Northampton – particularly as the splendid Clive Swift is cast in the role of Whittlestaff. Alas, it was not to be. Snow stopped play – or rather my getting to it – but that doesn't mean the fortunate people who live thereabouts shouldn't flock to it in their thousands.

By lucky chance, carrying emergency rations and a compass, I had earlier in the week travelled out to Richmond to see a revival of Alan Ayckbourn's *Confusions*, a play which had its premiere in Scarborough in 1974. This particular production started last year at the Gateway Theatre, Chester, has been touring ever since with a break for Christmas – and is due, once the run is over in Richmond, to go to Chichester, Guildford, Windsor and Poole.

*Confusions* is composed of five separate one-act playlets performed by a company of five, each playing many parts, not all successfully but mostly with style and panache. The first play, Mother Figure, about a harassed young woman, housebound and child-bound and burdened with a husband who's playing away from home, is the best, at least in my opinion, being very, very funny indeed. Joanna Myers as the mother left too long alone in the company of children and no longer able or willing to spot the difference between babies and adults, alternately disciplining and soothing the unfortunate neighbours and only capable of conversing in outrageous baby-talk, gives an hilarious yet always real performance.

The rest of the cast – Vincent Brimble, Graham Seed, Christopher Timothy and Rula Lénska – are equally excellent. Many mature women in the audience were laughing so much they had to use handkerchiefs. I made a mental note that the very next time I took a car drive into the country I would resist pointing out either moo-cows or baa-lambs to my elderly companions.

The other four playlets, dealing with a fraught dinner encounter, an unsuccessful seduction attempt, a group of self-sacrificial characters in the park and a disastrous garden party, were pretty funny too, just not as funny. That Miss Lenska can look glamorous and elegant is hardly surprising; that she can appear dowdy and even common is something of a feat. She also has perfect comic timing and is, on occasions, moving. Once or twice I thought Christopher Timothy was pushing for effect a little too hard, and Vincent Brimble and Graham Seed both blotted their copybook a tiny bit when one went too far as a silly-billy Cub master, the other as a too-camp vicar. Still, it must be hard to rein in when the audience is loving every minute and practically begging you to go over the top. The laughter was tremendous, the applause terrific, the evening memorable. One can't say fairer than that.

# Cat and Mouse (Sheep)

## The Gate, April 1996

It was J. B. Priestley who, sometime in the 60s, wrote that Western man is now schizophrenic. He argued that though the writer and dramatist was the instrument of whatever there is in the general deep unconscious, unfortunately what he produced was of little interest to the mass of people most in danger of losing their true individuality to the collectives of our time. If the pronouncement had been made by anyone other than Priestley, a man with his feet on the ground if ever there was one, I'd have dismissed it as arty-farty.

The Gate exists to introduce the work of international playwrights to a British audience. It has a small, deep stage next door to a pub in Notting Hill and is presenting a season of plays from the continent. I went to see *Cat and Mouse (Sheep)* by Gregory Motton, a UK playwright, whose previous work, although seen at the Royal Court, is not much appreciated here. The French regard him highly and this play had its premiere at the Odéon Theatre in Paris. It was received with acclaim and described as a libertarian piece of theatre, destructive, plebeian, leaving no trace after its passage except the strong weeds of its sarcasm.

The play has six characters and four actors and the action takes place in a small grocery shop run by Uncle, Aunty and their nephew Gengis. In Paris the part of Gengis was played by a man. Here, it's played by the actress Rudi Davies (my daughter!), who gives a performance which is unnervingly innocent and threatening. It doesn't matter that she looks very much like a young female, because Aunty, superbly acted by Penelope Diamond, says she's a man and the very masculine Uncle of Tony Rohr is discovered to be a lady when Gengis rapes him.

If this sounds too much to take, bear with me. There is nothing in the programme notes to indicate why the characters look one thing and turn out to be something else, or indeed any clue as to what the author thinks the play is about, but that doesn't matter either because it's extremely theatrical and satirical. Within the first few minutes Uncle assumes the voice of the people, many people, and spews out a long, poetic diatribe beginning: 'Your Aunty, she's always been a swinger . . . but I'm more your man with a book beside the fire, a bit of an intellectual, a rearguard man, a thinker, a political animal. . . . I'm left wing, I'm anti-semitic, I'm anti this, I'm anti that, I'm a star-fucker and I'm interested in crystal balls . . . and things you stick on the fridge and notes and notelets and I live in London because there's a thriving bisexual community there. . . . I don't read much but I like a good book about suffering Chinese or suffering anybody . . .'. Uncle is a wonderful part for an actor and Rohr rises to it magnificently.

The play ends with Gengis, having taken over the world, being deposed by Uncle and stood on a chair with a rope round his neck. He asks Auntie a series of questions: 'What happens when my back begins to bleed?' 'Then you are dead and dead indeed.' 'What happens when the cat's away?' 'The mice begin to play.' Aunty tiptoes off and Gengis says flatly, 'Aunty, I'm frightened.'

Comparisons may be odious, but to my mind Motton is Pinter in reverse, Orton accelerated and T. S. Eliot brought up to date. The play will be out of production by the time you read this, but a copy of the script is available in the Methuen Drama series.

# *Jolson*

## Victoria Palace, May 1996

In the '30s, Al Jolson became the highest-paid entertainer in the United States, earning somewhere around $17,000 a week. By the '40s he was considered old-hat. But in 1946 there was a revival of his popularity when Hollywood made a film of his life, Larry Parks acting the role but Jolson himself on the soundtrack. I saw the film, shortly after it was released, one Saturday afternoon at the Palace cinema in Southport, and I do remember thinking that there was a mismatch between the face on screen and the voice that came out of its mouth; the lips moved at the right pace but the eyes weren't right.

One Wednesday a couple of weeks ago I went to a matinée at the Victoria Palace of *Jolson*, winner of the 1996 Laurence Olivier Award for Best Musical of 1996. The theatre was packed out with charabanc parties. I wasn't expecting a great deal owing to a review I'd read carping on about how there wasn't much of a storyline, that it was a mere linking together of episodic cameos enlivened by tunes well known to a wartime generation. Either the critic in question was world-weary or else brain-dead from too many first-night performances, because quite simply this was magic time, as that Hun in the helmet said in the Mel Brooks film, *The Producers*.

Take the sets, for instance – the dressing room, the restaurant, the New York skyline backdrop, the breathtaking finale inside Radio City, the '50s big band rising in tiers to a backcloth of stars and each step of the stairway bordered with glittering lights. I thought the mansion set in *Sunset Boulevard* was terrific enough, but I now realize it swamped the action, whereas in *Jolson* the scenery is part of the whole. As for its being episodic – what musical isn't? And in fact the book in this one was remarkable for its sense of continuity and I never felt it was being manipulated to get in a song.

And then, of course, there's Brian Conley as Jolson, giving a performance which defies description. Quite literally, one can't take one's eyes off him. Every movement, that odd stiff-kneed walk with the bum stuck out – James Cagney had it too, and Cicely Courtneidge – every gesture, every inflection of his voice brings Jolson superbly to life. The eyes are absolutely right – sort of dead, like Archie Rice in *The Entertainer*. All the cast rise with him, particularly John Bennet as his agent. I seem to remember I was in Dundee Rep with Mr Bennet a very long time ago. Then there's John Conroy as Frankie Holmes; he and Conley belt out together 'The Spaniard That Blighted My Life' and bring the house down, as they say.

There's a kind of politically correct apology in the programme notes to do with singers blacking up on stage. I do wish they wouldn't do that sort of thing; it's so damn patronizing. Actually, I think there was only one scene when this Jolson did black up, and it was at the beginning. He certainly didn't at the magnificent and spectacular end when he sank to his knees singing 'Mammy'. Enough. Just go and see it.

# Passion

## Queen's Theatre, June 1996

I received two letters the other week from readers who wanted to know why this column seems, recently, to concentrate on musicals rather than straight plays. I can only plead that, as *The Oldie* is a monthly magazine, it would appear sensible to attend performances of theatrical shows that are likely to be still running by the time the review goes to press. This mostly rules out fringe plays and often those in repertory at the National. A straight play tends not to run as long as a musical, either because the star gets sick of doing the same thing night after night or because the mainly tourist audience likes a spot of singalong to break up the words.

So – yet again I went last week to a play with music, namely Stephen Sondheim's *Passion*, now showing at the Queen's Theatre, Shaftesbury Avenue. Though aware of his reputation as a breaker of new ground, I didn't think I'd ever seen a show of his until I read in the programme notes that he'd written *Sweeney Todd*, which I saw years ago and didn't think very musical.

Two things happened at the matinée performance of *Passion* which I attended. One, a snippet of conversation overheard from two ladies sitting behind me: 1st lady: 'He just sits down at the piano and begins to play.' 2nd lady: 'And what does she do?' 1st lady: 'She just strips naked and gets on the swing.' A riveting insight into domestic life as lived in the provinces. The second remark was made by a very nice chap who approached me in the interval and kindly said he liked my reviews in *The Oldie* and where did I think *Passion* was coming from, or words to that effect.

Neither of us knew, but both agreed we weren't likely to burst into song the following morning.

The story behind the book is real. Originally called Fosca, it derives from an autobiographical novel written in serial form by an Italian called Tarchetti who died before he could complete it at the age of 29. His best friend finished it off, and it's about obsessional love. Giorgio, a captain in the army, loves Clara, a married woman, and she loves him. Giorgio is sent away to join a regiment stationed in an arid landscape somewhere at the foot of the Alps.

His commanding officer has a sick cousin – Fosca – who screams day and night and falls in love with Giorgio. The regimental doctor plays Devil's Advocate and urges Giorgio to be kind to her, as she may die very soon. He, Giorgio, is a good man and goes along with it, mainly because his love for Clara is unsatisfactory.

Actually, I now see why Sondheim is so wonderful. I didn't hear any music; I just got involved with the plot and, contrary to most every other play one sees, the second act was better than the first. This, of course, had much to do with Michael Ball as Giorgio and Maria Friedman as Fosca. They are both utterly believable and triumphant in their roles, as is the rest of the cast.

All in all it's a very tragic play, which is stimulating for an audience if the piece manages to remain constant in its narrative drive, which this does. It's not a fun two hours but it is provoking and dramatic.

# Romeo and Juliet

## Barbican, September 1996

It's quite possible that the Barbican is the ugliest interior of any building in London. Its concrete walls, some arbitrarily and liberally embedded with pebble dash, its lumpy lighting fixtures and extraordinary golden 'thingies' perched on top of cheap partitions, send shivers down the spine. I suppose the pebbles are useful when it comes to striking matches, and, seeing smoking is allowed in the vicinity of the bar and there wasn't an ashtray in sight, quite handy when one needs to stub out a cigarette. I think the chaps who 'designed' the foyer must have hated the theatre; possibly as babies they had mothers who trod the boards while leaving them in the care of tipsy landladies.

Since I last visited the building the artistic talents of a party of brush-wielding nursery school infants have obviously been employed to brighten up certain areas; the resulting splattering of rosy pink, blue and purple paint is positively uplifting. It's also an eye-opener these days to observe what is considered suitable attire for a night out at the theatre. Unless football hooligans have taken to going to Shakespearian plays, it only goes to show that you can't judge a man just because he wears his baseball cap the wrong way round.

Once inside the auditorium and the lights having dimmed, all was forgiven. Transported to the pavement cafe in Verona, we watched a squabble flare up between the Capulets and the Montagues; the RSC had begun their performance of the Adrian Noble production of *Romeo and Juliet*.

Within five minutes it became evident that this was indeed a company, in the sense of the old repertory system.

It's true that we were under the spell of the piercing 'oldie' lights of Julian Glover, Christopher Benjamin, Susan Brown, Gary Taylor and Jeffery Dench in the roles of Friar Laurence, Capulet, Nurse, Peter and Montague, but the younger members of the cast did them proud. Zubin Varla as Romeo and Lucy Whybrow as Juliet, looked and behaved like children, which is as it should be. They all shone, Tybalt and Paris – though I didn't like his moustache – Lady Capulet and the waiters. At one point tears came to my eyes, the moment when the impetuous Romeo stabbed horrible cousin Capulet.

I read *Romeo and Juliet* at school, and her speech in her bedroom when she's about to take the medicine which will feign death – 'What if it be a poison, which the friar subtly hath administered to have me dead, lest in this marriage he should be dishonoured, because he married me before to Romeo' – was my chosen speech when I auditioned for the lead in Preminger's film of Joan of Arc. No, I didn't get it.

It's a lovely production and not at all long. And there's music too. At one point the street minstrels launched into the tune of Just One Cornetto and such was the spell we were under there was hardly a titter. What more can one say?

# Two Gentlemen of Verona

## Globe Theatre, October 1996

I took a taxi to Sam Wanamaker's Globe Theatre on Saturday night. The cab driver didn't know where it was any
more than I did, but, having crossed some bridge or other
and stopped to make endless enquiries we wound in and out
of deserted streets and drew up outside a building site
pressed by crowds. My companion and I had intended to
dine before the play. Alas, there was a makeshift café across
the road supplying the dreaded carrot cake and coffee.
There wasn't a pub in sight. Why, in all these intervening
years, hasn't some enterprising publican erected a watering
hole called the Henry IV or the Hamlet Arms?

There was a terrific air of excitement among the punters
kept outside the entrances, and when at last the barriers
were taken down and we poured on to the 'going to be'
piazza and glimpsed the cream outline of the building,
thatched roof dark against the white sky, there rose a gasp of
anticipation. Once up some concrete steps we entered the
actual theatre, a glorious circular edifice constructed of
green oak which isn't green at all but the colour of milk –
open to the heavens across which soared the arm of an
equally glorious scarlet crane, its grappling chain hanging
like some gigantic hangman's noose above the pagoda
structure arching the stage. The plaster for the walls, the
programme tells one, is made of sand, lime and goats' hair.
There's an open space where the poor can stand (tickets £5)
with straw on the floor to mop up the rain.

Those with seats can hire cushions for a pound a go –
green oak is rather hard on the bum. The whole thing is
wonderful . . . breathtaking. What a triumph, and God bless

Wanamaker for his dream and the National Lottery for coughing up some money at the end.

Soon enough Shakespeare began, or rather the *Two Gentlemen of Verona*. Shakespeare and his outpourings of genius are what this new accurate copy of the old Globe theatre is all about. It's presumed to be his first play, written sometime between 1590 and 1595, and I gathered the plot concerns crossed love and women disguising themselves as men in order to get their man.

I never got into it. Instead, I was fascinated by the arm of the crane, the way its scribble of wires and elegant super-structure began to stand out against a sky turning from zinc white to cobalt blue.

Beneath, the young actors shouted to make themselves heard and jerked about like marionettes. Too often, feign-ing ecstasy, they flung themselves to the ground and writhed about. Most of my lack of attention was down to the fact that they were dressed in modern clothes. How could we be sitting in a thatched, green oak 16th-century theatre when the characters were prancing about in city suits and little summer dresses? Why did two of them speak with transatlantic accents? Why did most of them walk as if they'd been sitting on green oak for far too long? But that's not all. I may be unfair, but it struck me that this was amateur night out. A parade of first-year drama students, steeped in television viewing, trying their best to be strolling players. I imagine Shakespeare was used to taking pot-luck, but Sam must be turning in his grave.

# Art

I switched on the wireless the other day in the middle of a swingeing attack by someone or other on the blandness of British theatre critics in comparison to their American counterparts. Michael Billington defended valiantly. For myself, having read Arnold Wesker on the subject of Broadway reviews and Peter Nichols on the 'closed shop' attitude of British theatre management, I can only say there doesn't seem to be much difference between the power exercised by critics and the clout wielded by producers – the first can run a play into the ground; the second ensures it never gets shown.

Fortunately, in the case of less intellectual offerings, Agatha Christie's *The Mousetrap* being a prime example, the public shows its muscle, as indeed it has for that superb dramatic piece, *An Inspector Calls*, by J. B. Priestley – whose prize-winning revival I hated – having seen it in repertory many years before, without gimmicks. Both offerings were first performed a long time ago, and I dare say those revisiting *The Mousetrap* after a gap of 35 years complain nostalgically that things ain't what they used to be. We are all programmed by our past and most of us see no necessity to view anything with a fresh eye. Trouble is, there used to be a repertory theatre in every town; in due course provincial audiences could see for themselves a French's acting edition version of a London production, which made for a public more knowledgeable about current dramatic trends.

I doubt that *Art*, a new play by Yasmina Reza, translated from the French by Christopher Hampton and now showing at Wyndham's Theatre, will ever need to be mucked about in the future. It could not be bettered. Though its plot may not be as easy to follow as that of *The Mousetrap*, or as profound as *An Inspector Calls*, it outshines both if you believe that a play should provoke as well as entertain.

*Art* concerns three men whose friendship is torn apart, or rather rearranged, by one of them spending a fortune on the purchase of a painting whose canvas, somewhat like the content of most plays, is nothing more than a blank square primed with white emulsion paint. I read an earlier review in which the critic argued that the piece didn't really work here because only Frenchmen could possibly get their knickers in a twist over a painting. As it's perfectly obvious from Hampton's translation that we are not in Blackpool – the Pompidou Centre is mentioned and the three characters are exotically named Marc, Yvan and Serge – I can't think what he was on about. Perhaps he thought the piece would be more accessible if the chaps fell out over football.

Serge owns the painting; he's been to all the exhibitions and digested all the modern-art books; he's been told what he likes. Marc has a nodding acquaintance with Art and knows what he likes; he's appalled at the price paid for the picture. Serge doesn't mind one way or the other; he just likes Yvan and Marc. It helps, of course, that Yvan, Serge and Marc are played by Ken Stott, Tom Courtenay, and Albert Finney. Finney blusters; Courtenay prances and appears the strongest; Stott cries and is the most lonely. To me, that is.

I'm uncomfortably aware that if the repertory system ever comes back and I saw the play again, I'd bemoan the fact that the actors didn't match up to the trio at Wyndham's. This is a wonderful play, particularly if you're suspicious of modern art, of modern anything.

# 1997

Death of Princess Diana, Robert Mitchum, James Stewart, Allen Ginsberg and Mother Teresa.

Edinburg scientists produce Dolly, the cloned sheep.

Tony Blair and the Labour party romp home in a landslide victory.

*Peter Pan* by James Barrie is about Lost Boys who won't grow up in a place called Never Never Land. Apart from the very first production when Captain Hook and Mr Darling were played by separate actors both parts are now performed by the same one. This is to show that a father is always a mixture of good and bad.

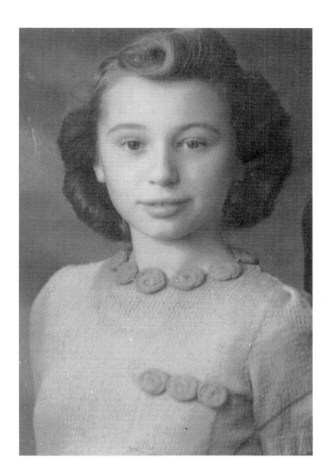

Myself when young

Tripping the light fantastic in Tring

Shorn of hair at the Liverpool Playhouse

Leaning over the door in *The Beaver Coat*

Examining a kipper with Mabel Constanduros

Me and Ken Barlow banning the bomb in *Coronation Street*

Attending to one's eyes in *Coronation Street*

Outside the Rover's Return years later

Herbert Jennings and friend pulling faces

Herbert Jennings at it again

Herbert Jennings
trying to smile

# Joey and Gina's Wedding

## Café Royal, January 1997

Although my dear friend Brodie and I speak to each other
via our answering machines at least once a fortnight, we
haven't met in the flesh for over a year. Last week my
machine said he was taking me to a wedding reception and
we must meet inside the foyer of the Café Royal. I got there
early and it was fascinating watching the revolving doors
whizz round and round discharging middle-aged chaps in
evening dress bound for various functions. The dialogue
between those waiting for partners to arrive and those
passing through was worthy of Rattigan. 'I know you' – this
from a beefy gent in one of those wonderful city coats with a
velvet collar upon spotting a diminutive fellow in a fluffy
evening shirt – 'You're an old Hillingdonian,' (possibly I
misheard) 'aren't you? You snivelled a lot, as I remember.'
'Yah, yah,' chortled the short fellow. 'Good of you to
remember.'

Brodie arrived soon after and escorted me to a side door
which led to a basement. Our tickets were in the form of an
invitation to the union of Regina Margarita Angelina
Granata (Gina), offspring of Italian East End parents and
Joseph James Anthony Milano Jar (Joey), an Italian-
American nurtured in Chicago. We entered the basement
at 7.15. At 7.20 the aunt of the bride, a widow dressed all in
black, sidled up to the bar and confided that she neither
approved of the Irish priest chosen to conduct the service
nor the bride's mother who was definitely an alcoholic.
Also, the sister of Joey was definitely 'on' something. Before
she could elaborate, the mother in question approached,
thanked us for coming and spoke emotionally for several

minutes about the tragic death of her husband, an ice-cream salesman who had died at the wheel of his van following an explosion which had torn it apart. He might have recovered from the blast if the ice cream pipe hadn't blown up and drowned him in its contents – a bit like that superb short story, 'Christ in Concrete'.

Soon after, the groom arrived and we were ushered to our seats in the Chapel of Love. I thought the priest was a dish and behaved very well when the altar decorations caught fire. All in all, it was a lovely service, what with the pretty bride, her handsome husband and the three riveting brides-maids, one of whom was the one 'on' something. The reception was spectacular – wonderful food, champagne, poetry readings, songs, several punch-ups involving the families of both bride and groom, and a marvellous band to which we rocked and rolled and danced the Hokey-Cokey until a quarter past eleven. Father McCarthy got dead drunk, goosed one of the bridesmaids and collapsed under the table before the wedding cake was cut, but not before Gina had tried to knife Joey; it was just a lovers' tiff. All in all, it was a typical wedding and a wonderful night out. You do have to get into the spirit of the thing, or rather imbibe as much spirit as you can lay hands on, in order to gain the maximum enjoyment, because this is something called interaction, and we all know how inhibiting that can be when cold sober. The show is created and directed by Jay Legget, produced by Robert Mackintosh and performed by a brilliant cast of 30. It's a treat.

# Peter Pan

## Yorkshire Playhouse, February 1997

Was there ever such a marvellous dramatic offering as *Peter Pan*? It was the first completely straight play for children and the only one that is also a great work of literature. Yet when its author, James Barrie, took it to the actor/manager Herbert Beerbohm Tree, hoping he would play Captain Hook, it was Tree's opinion that Barrie had gone out of his mind. Fortunately the impresario Charles Frohman, who later went down on the *Lusitania*, realized its magic and on Boxing Day, 1904, the curtain went up to reveal those windows in the nursery of the Darling household. I've read a description of that momentous occasion – the first few moments of surprise as the sophisticated audience listened to those childish voices, smiled indulgently as Nana shuffled in with the medicine, and then, of course, Tinkerbell began her crazy dance across the backcloth, the windows opened and Peter came flying in from the stars.

In the next 50 years the play was performed more than 10,000 times. Much has been written hinting at the unhealthy interest Barrie was supposed to have shown in young children, but miraculously, even in our own cynical and sensational age none of the flung-mud has ever stuck. *Peter Pan* remains the stupendous spinning, by a master craftsman, of make-believe.

Last month I went to see it at the West Yorkshire Playhouse in Leeds, performed by a young company directed by the brilliant, also young, Matthew Warchus, he who recently directed *Volpone* for the Royal National Theatre and *Art* at Wyndham's, and who is currently preparing *Falstaff* for Opera North and *Hamlet* for the RSC. Warchus's superb control of crowds – the battle between Tiger Lily's Indians and Hook's pirates, the dance of the Braves, the preparation for the walking of the plank – is equalled by his sensitive handling of a solitary Peter kicking soap bubbles, a penitent Tootles discovering he's shot Wendy and poor old Mr Darling putting a brave face on it at having to take on the Lost Boys.

Technically, this production is sensational, what with the music, the huge waltzing crocodile, the narrator's voice echoing round the auditorium, the flying children, the pirate ship with the waves dancing ahead. The designer, Rob Howell is possibly a genius, also the lighting chap, Hugh Vanstone. Dramatically, the production couldn't be bettered. I have heard that it may come to the National in two years' time. Costs are against it. It occurs to me that all those millions – our money – intended to be squandered on building that upturned pudding plate in Greenwich would be much better spent on sending this particular production to every theatre left in England. For our children's sake. For the sake of that awfully big adventure – God help us – the 21st century.

# Henry IV

## Old Vic, March 1997

Whenever, in this column, I find myself out of my depth in regards to dramatic criticism, I leaf through the great Harold Hobson's 1948 book on first nights at the theatre. Alter all, if any man knew what he was talking about, he did. Last week, after going to see *Henry IV* at the Old Vic and consulting Hobson's index, I was dismayed to find it contained not a single reference to this magnificent play. In fact, the only passing mention to Shakespeare comes in a diary entry a page before the appendix: 'Wed 31st Dec, 1947; To Dilys and Leonard Russell's customary New Year's Eve party, which is now as much an institution as New Year itself. ... At dinner sat next to Michael Redgrave ... introduced myself with the words, "You won't want to know me. I wrote a very uncomplimentary review of your performance in *Macbeth*." To which he replied promptly "I never read it".'

From schooldays, all I remember, in my skull, of *Henry IV*, is the King declaiming: 'When I from France set foot at Ravensburg.' The reason this somewhat unremarkable line remains with me is on account of my childhood address, 47 Ravenmeols Lane; such a small leap in word endings is neither here nor there.

*Henry IV*, at the Old Vic, is performed by the English Touring Company, which, in these days of cuts, means that the actors are paid twopence for their labour. It wasn't much different in the past, especially for the youngsters – at Liverpool in the 1950s I remained unpaid for two years, and, in the following year, received the equivalent, in today's terms, of monies sufficient to nurture a canary. That the superb and experienced actor Timothy West should travel round the country playing Falstaff makes cowards of us all. As the old sot, lecher and coward his is a wonderful performance, grizzled, rumbustious, touching. He works the stage; rolls the language round the auditorium. His son Sam, who plays Hal, is very good indeed and will be even better.

There are three other proper actors, Gary Waldhorn, Paul Imbusch and Joseph O'Connor. The rest, doubling up on roles, do their best, but the standard isn't high. It has much to do with the speaking of the Queen's English. Not many of us, in our dotage, approve of the manners, intonations or attitudes of a modern generation, and few of the present young, their hearing blasted to hell by rap 'music', are aware that their vowels are distorted. I blame such deficiency on our schools, which, for 100 years, have seen fit to drop the teaching of elocution from the curriculum.

Actually, by the time we got to Part II, the play swept me along and I stopped being so critical. I swear I had tears in my eyes when the King, on his way to becoming a 'successful man' and hailed by Falstaff – 'God save thee, my sweet boy', replies: 'I know thee not, old man.' The marvellous thing about Falstaff is that though he's a wicked old opportunist, he's never as rotten or inhuman as the others.

# The School for Wives

## Piccadilly Theatre, April 1997

*The School for Wives*, now showing at Piccadilly Theatre, was first performed in 1662 in France, its author, Molière, being a Frenchman. It is witty, bawdy, perceptive and ultimately gentle. It's interesting to note that in Britain, the playwright Wycherley was presenting the public with comedies so coarse and indecent and yet so savagely scornful of the vices of the day that he was labelled a 'moralist at heart'. He was obviously influenced by Molière because his best known work, *The Country Wife*, has almost the same plot as *The School for Wives*. In a month in which a prize-winning author has been accused of re-working a novel by Faulkner, it's worth mentioning that Molière pinched his plot from an earlier short story translated from the Spanish.

A middle-aged gent, dismayed at the regularity with which men are cuckolded by their wives, adopts a child of four and has her brought up in a convent. She is to be taught nothing of life beyond a little needlework. When she emerges, at last, to be his bride, he gleefully notes that she is a complete simpleton. Some weeks before the wedding he installs her in the grounds of his estate in a cottage staffed by a rustic couple – Carmen Silvera and Eric Sykes. It's not just that Sykes is a comedian and has superb timing, more that his body appears to dangle on invisible strings irretrievably tangled – he's out of control. His mouth says things that the rest of him contradicts. Silvera stays on the ground, so to speak, mainly because of her bosoms, but she threatens anarchy and has a terrific voice. It says much for Peter Bowles, playing Arnolphe, the bridegroom, that he more than holds his own. His expression of interest –

eyes held from spinning in their sockets, mouth rigidly curved as young Horace confides how the bride locked up in the cottage invited him to her bedroom – is inspirational. And he does convey that he's not a bad chap, that he does in the end realize that love will find a way. Misguided he may be, but never malicious. He's also got very nice legs.

As for Henry McGee, playing Amolphe's friend, mouth opening like a ventriloquist's doll, eyebrows on the go, he's the perfect side-kick. This is the stuff of comedy, not farce, though I'm not sure where the distinction lies unless it's something to do with character – in particular that of Agnes, beautifully performed by Gillian Keamey. Agnes is very real, very believable.

This is not a play overshadowed by a tremendous and technical set, scenery whizzing up and down stage, whirling round and round. At any rate, if it did, I didn't notice, which is as it should be.

I don't often go to evening performances, not liking to miss the nightly soaps. I must say that the West End is an eye-opener, what with the crowded streets, the roaring youth, crocodile queues outside the clubs, the inebriated customers rolling out of the pubs. Nothing changes, does it?

# Tom & Clem

## Aldwych Theatre, June 1997

*Tom & Clem*, written by Stephen Churchett, directed by Richard Wilson and starring two great actors at the height of their powers, must not be missed at the Aldwych Theatre. Michael Gambon plays Tom Driberg and Alec McCowan plays Clement Attlee. The two other members of the cast, Daniel de la Falaise as the excitable Alexei, and Sarah Woodward as the coolly competent Kitty, are also excellent.

Of the two events that form the background to the play – the Potsdam Conference and the general election of 1945 – the first shaped Europe and the second the Britain of the last half of this century. Driberg was an MP, a homosexual, an outstanding 'radical left' journalist and something of a wag, though not necessarily in that order. According to Woodrow Wyatt's splendid autobiography, *Confessions of an Optimist*, after Driberg had pointed out that the Speaker's announcement at the end of Question Time – 'The Clerk will now proceed to reader the Orders of the Day' – fitted the tune of 'The Battle Hymn of the Republic', both men set up a spirited humming whenever the occasion arose.

In the play, Driberg comes across as emotional, cock-obsessed and reliant on the bottle – but he's arrived in Potsdam straight from reporting on the liberation of a concentration camp and he can't wipe the images of the dead from his eyes. Such is the strength of Gambon in the role that we see Driberg as he must have been all those years ago, at a time when drink and homosexuality invariably spelt weakness, loneliness and a tottering descent along the path to hell. Not that Gambon totters; for a heavily built man – not fat – he's very light on his feet. One might almost call it dancing, something akin to the delicate prancing of Zero Mostel and Charles Laughton. It's with awe that I record that Mr Gambon, many years back, performed in a television play of mine. One scene was shot in our street and, between takes, he and Rosemary Leach sat in my kitchen out of the cold. There were floodlights outside, and David Lean arrived in a limousine and watched on the corner.

Clem Attlee, on the other hand, that formidable leader of old Labour, is everyone's dad of the period; mine anyway, though without the moustache. He's very conscientious and worthy, but so prim. When he lets on to a knowledge of Driberg's predisposition for lavatory encounters, he's tart rather than smart in his remarks; when he climbs onto that table and sings that song it's no wonder Driberg looks so anxious – one fears Clem will do himself an injury. And yet, it was his signature of parliamentary papers that gave birth to the Welfare State, once such a blessing. It was his disciplined copper-plate that changed society, not the tear-stained copy of those such as Driberg, whose words, however emotive, moved the intelligentsia rather than touched the poor. I still feel sorry for Churchill, slung out after winning the war and referred to throughout my childhood as that 'rotten privileged swine', but I don't have any feelings about Mr Attlee, beyond recognizing that he was a decent man. Decent men usually merge into the background, don't they? It's the buggers one remembers.

# Life Support

## Aldwych Theatre, September 1997

I waited for a few days before writing this review, because I wondered whether my reaction to the play in question – *Life Support* by Simon Gray, now showing at the Aldwych Theatre – would be different or more favourable, after a lapse of time. It isn't, though at the matinée I went to, the audience was extremely attentive and appreciative. In part, this was due to the excellent performances, particularly that of Alan Bates as JG, the guilt-ridden husband. The fault, I think, lies in the structure of the play.

It opens in the private room of an English hospital, with a woman lying motionless on the bed. There are cables attached to her, so we know it's an intensive care job, not measles or anything simple. A male voiceover, sonorous and solemn, delivers an 'if only' monologue. The woman is in a coma, the result of having persuaded her husband, JG, a travel writer of repute, to take her on a fact-finding trip to foreign parts – he usually left her at home. Sitting in a distant field, a bee stung her on the neck, a sting from which she's unlikely to recover. JG stays with her night and day, talking to her, stroking her hand, discussing their past lives together. Both of them had something of a drink problem, but apparently gave it up. JG's brother, a failed actor, visits as does his lady agent, and a doctor attached to the ward who's studying the reaction of relatives under stress. The brother is after money, the agent needs contracts signed, and the doctor needs material for his thesis. The scenes with the brother are very well done and raised the only belly laugh of the afternoon. The one in which the lady agent admits she and JG had, and still are having, an affair doesn't work. It's stage-managed, of course, to shock the wife out of her coma, but I doubt if the news would have come as a surprise.

Still, the first three-quarters of an hour passed interestingly enough, but after that things definitely dragged. In part, this was due to the irritating device of the voiceover – I couldn't work out whether JG was doing a stream of consciousness or reading from one of his books – and the rest down to the cause, eventually explained, of his angst.

Far from sitting in a foreign field when the bee zoomed in, they were drinking in the street and possibly having a flaming row. 'Ow, Ow,' wails the wife, clutching at her neck, at which a soldier rushes up, pushes her to the ground, pulls out first his gun, then his prick and strains to pee on her face. JG, ignorant of the healing properties of urine where bee stings are concerned, knocks him away.

He does love his wife, the audience is convinced of that, and he's already informed us that usually, when fact-finding alone, he stays in his hotel room and uses guide books and imagination. But his guilt doesn't really make sense. Most husbands wouldn't take kindly to a military man using their wife as a loo. Besides, we're never there when anything happens. Think of the scene in *Death of a Salesman* where Biff finds his father in bed with a tart, or that moment on the blasted heath when Lear goes mad in a thunderstorm. We're shown it happening. In *Life Support* we just get told about it afterwards.

# *The Herbal Bed*

## Duchess Theatre, October 1997

In 1607, Shakespeare's elder daughter, Susanna, married John Hall, a noted physician. Some five years later she was slandered by John Lane, who had been dismissed from his post as assistant to Hall. He was a boozer, a womanizer and afraid of his father. Sweet on Susanna, and rebuffed by her – he said she kissed him on the stairs, she said she'd pushed him away – he later told the drinkers in the local pub that he knew for a fact she was having an affair with Rafe Smith, a haberdasher of Sheep Street, Stratford. Worse, if possible, he claimed he had caught her mixing a medicinal potion, for herself, made up of ingredients used in the treatment of venereal disease. Susanna, urged on by her husband, brought a charge of defamation against Lane in the diocesan court at Worcester Cathedral. These are the historical facts on which Peter Whelan has based his brilliant play, The *Herbal Bed*, now performing at the Duchess Theatre.

Those convinced that a drama set in the 17th century must, by definition, be somewhat stuffy, full of posturings and antiquated language, are in for a surprise. While remaining within the spirit of its age, *The Herbal Bed* is nonetheless a psychological tour de force and utterly relevant to the present time.

For one thing, Susanna is guilty of adultery, in thought if not in deed. She attempts to seduce the haberdasher, and would certainly have succeeded if the maid hadn't come back unexpectedly. Rafe, though hopelessly in love with Susanna, is grateful for the intrusion. He's a good man and respects Dr Hall. So does Susanna, but her husband is reserved and lacking in passion, or so she makes us believe.

Her character, naturalistically and beautifully played by Kate Duchene, is complex; she's intelligent, kind and exceedingly manipulative, though in the nicest way and possibly for the right reasons. She persuades Rafe to lie about being in the house alone with her, by convincing him that a scandal would ruin the doctor and thus cause suffering to the poor among his patients. She gets the maid to lie by promising to look upon her as a friend rather than a servant, and she means it.

The power of this play resides in the way one keeps changing one's mind about its characters. Take the doctor, magnificently performed by Mick Ford. Having questioned his wife about whether there is any truth in the slander, he appears wholly satisfied with her reply. Then, later on, I began to believe that he knew it was otherwise, and that his pretence was because he loved her and felt she had cause to be unfaithful. Then again, perhaps he was going along with it so as to hold onto his practice. And perhaps Jack Lane, the cause of all the trouble, wasn't lying about the kissing on the stairs. Daniel Ryan, as Jack, was certainly convincing when he told the story. Indeed, all the actors were convincing, and the court scene a blazing triumph.

I won't give away the explanation about the medicine Susanna was preparing. Suffice to say, in the closing scene she is expecting her sick father.

I reviewed the highly successful play *Art* not long ago and found it delightful. After seeing *The Herbal Bed*, I have come to the conclusion that it was thin, slick and empty.

# Lecture on the Crimean War

## Hunterian Museum, December 1997

By the time you read this we will all be involved in the dubious merriment leading up to Christmas, so I did think I would pop out to view a jolly pantomime, one suitable for oldie grandchildren. Alas, *Peter Pan*, coming on at the National, is not yet ready, nor could I find *Puss in Boots* listed, an entertainment I last saw with Dorothy Ward in the leading role. I have not, even at this distance in time, forgotten Miss Ward slapping her splendid thighs and uttering the immortal line, 'What! 12 miles to London and still no sign of Dick.'

Instead, I decided to review one of a series of lectures organized by the Royal College of Surgeons, given last Tuesday in the lecture theatre below the awesome Hunterian Museum, which houses, among other splendid exhibits, the Irish giant. There were three talks, the first on surgery at Waterloo, the second on surgery during the Crimean War and the third bringing us up to date on medical advances between World Wars I and II. I was especially interested in the Crimean lecture, since I am rushing towards the end of a novel which features the Battle of Inkerman, but found Mr Kenneth Cumplin's dissertation on Waterloo equally fascinating. Did you know, for instance, that even then they understood the danger of stitching up a wound too tightly, thus trapping pus and encouraging infection? Or, that Napoleon died, not of arsenic in the wallpaper of St Helena but from cancer in the region of the bowel, an affliction that carried off his father before him?

The Crimean War began in 1854 and was over by '56. Of the 20,000-odd British casualties, only 4,000 died of wounds sustained in battle. The rest perished from cholera, dysentery, syphilis and frostbite. The slides were particularly informative, including the first war photograph of an amputation, taking place in what looked like a cowshed.

If one got shot in the stomach by a bit of cannon ball, the death rate was 100 per cent; loss of fingers, 0.5 per cent; amputation of legs and arms – here we were shown a heap of them kicking and pointing at the sky – somewhere around 40 per cent. Of course, it wasn't so much the sawing-off that killed, for chloroform was then in use, as the rat-infested hospitals in which the injured convalesced. Stomach injuries were fatal, because no one knew how to put the intestines back in.

Inkerman was known as the Soldiers' Battle. It began in dense fog at five in the morning, when 40,000 Russians made a surprise attack. On account of the visibility, or lack of it, it was hand-to-hand slaughter by bayonet. In some cases the dead of both sides lay like bracelets, linked together by steel.

The surgeons themselves sat exams and had to have seven years' experience of hospital wards. They were required to pay for their own boots and provide their own instruments. We were shown a drawing of a surgeon wearing a leather apron and carrying a bloodletting bowl and a tin of leeches.

All in all, it was a fun night out, and the lectures at the College, one a month, continue until 24 March. The subjects include 'Vascular Surgery' and 'Transplantation of the Kidneys'.

Merry Christmas and God Bless Us Every One.

# 1998

Death of Ted Hughes, Catherine Cookson, Enoch Powell, Frank Sinatra, Joan Dickson and terrorist Pol Pot.

ITV *News at Ten* to be scrapped.

President Saddam Hussein announces a Holy War against sanctions imposed by the UN.

*Oh! What a Lovely War* is about war-games, the stupidity of generals, the profiteering of weapon manufacturers and the ignorance of the public.

# A Letter of Resignation

## Comedy Theatre, February 1998

> Sexual intercourse began
> In nineteen sixty-three
> (Which was rather late for me) –
> Between the end of the Chatterley ban
> And the Beatles' first LP.

So wrote Philip Larkin, sometime after the Profumo affair, although I seem to remember it starting months before with a photograph of a headless man.

They were giddy times; never before had my father, a product of the Edwardian age, returned from his commercial travelling and told so many jokes at the expense of his betters. The laughter only stopped – for me, not my Dad – with the publication of *Private Eye*, with its shaming cartoon depicting Stephen Ward being carried dying on a stretcher under the caption 'For God's sake say something, even if it's only Goodbye'.

Hugh Whitemore's play, *A Letter of Resignation*, showing until the end of February at the Comedy Theatre, is set in the library of a castle in Scotland one evening in 1963. The Prime Minister, Harold Macmillan, and his wife, Lady Dorothy, are attending a party to celebrate the retirement of an old retainer. In the middle of the festivities Macmillan's private secretary arrives, closely followed by a chap from MI5.

The private secretary has brought John Profumo's letter admitting that he lied to the House when he denied sleeping with Christine Keeler. The man from MI5 is on hand to assure the PM that Stephen Ward can be made the scapegoat and that the police are prepared to prosecute him on a trumped-up charge of living on immoral earnings.

For those few among you who may not recall the facts of the Profumo scandal, suffice it to say that it involved a pretty girl, the Secretary of State for War, a Russian naval officer, Lord Astor and an osteopath. Macmillan resigned, Profumo went on to help the poor, and the osteopath committed suicide.

Nothing much happens in the play. There is no forward development, simply a telling of what has already taken place. This, tackled by a lesser playwright with a less fascinating story to tell, might have produced something of a non-starter. In Hugh Whitemore's skilful hands it becomes an absorbing and thought-provoking drama which grips from beginning to end.

There's a piece in the middle when we have a flashback to Lady Dorothy confessing to Macmillan that she is pregnant by Bob Boothby. Harold's reaction to this distressing news is both moving and dignified. There's something terribly sweet about him, which is possibly to do with the superb performance given by Edward Fox. I say possibly, because for most of the time I thought it was Macmillan up there on the stage and not an actor at all. It wasn't just the voice or the walk or the make-up, but a mysterious inner force that made me believe I was in the presence of a good and honourable man, even if he did keep referring to Miss Keeler as a tart. And I was touched rather than made indignant by his conviction that lying to the House was worse than adultery.

Clare Higgins as Lady Dorothy was equally real. I reckon she was the ideal mate for Harold and now understand – which I never did before – how a rather stout lady in tweeds was capable of arousing such passion.

# An Enemy of the People

## National Theatre, June 1998

There are some plays one cannot forget, for the performances or the pieces themselves, the sets or the brilliance of the direction. Very few productions achieve all four elements of excellence. But in Ibsen's *An Enemy of the People*, now showing at the National Theatre, such a miracle has been accomplished. The entire Labour Government should see it, for it vindicates the need for money for the Arts, and shows the British theatre in full and glorious flower.

Ibsen wrote the play in 1882, before *The Wild Duck* and after *Ghosts*, the latter being received with such a frenzied display of outrage – its subject matter dealt with hereditary syphilis – that it is easy to see how Ibsen temporarily identified with the persecuted central character of *An Enemy of the People*. Yet, being the genius he was, he saw both sides of the dilemma of the thinking minority at the mercy of the majority. His ideas, abstracted from his dramas, were not in themselves boldly original or revolutionary. As J. B. Priestley observed, he was neither a Nietzsche nor a Marx, merely a dramatist. The insight he offered stemmed not from being a critic of society but from his own personality, his own conflicts and stresses, for he was a man bitterly divided and exiled from the only land he cared for, his native Norway.

In *An Enemy of the People*, Stockmann, a doctor and scientist, discovers that the waters of the spa town in which he lives are contaminated with bacteria. His solution to the problem is simple – inform the townsfolk, close the baths, purify the water and lay new pipes. He has every expectation of being congratulated for his timely spotting of the trouble and his understanding of the problem. Alas, he has not taken into account the feelings of that other minority, the investors, the Town Council and the property developers who stand to lose money by such a revelation. Nor has he thought out the attitudes of an ignorant majority who depend for their daily bread on the commerce of the rich. Sticking to his guns, sure he is in the right, convinced that truth will be triumphant, all too soon he becomes an enemy of the people.

Ian McKellen's performance as Stockmann is shattering. He's so hopeful, so nervy, so confident of the common sense of his fellow men, with a head so full of ideas that he can't keep still. Only towards the end, when he finally realizes he can't win and understands the power of the ignorance surging to engulf him, does he become still, almost calm. This a truly great performance.

As for the rest of the cast – Charlotte Cornwell as his wife, Isabel Pollen as his daughter, Stephen Moore as his brother, Ralph Nossek as his father-in-law, Pip Donaghy as Aslaksen, Paul Higgins as Hovstad – all are wonderful.

To see the work of a great director in action, at the height of his powers, witness Trevor Nunn's handling of Ibsen. What control, what insight! Never before have I been to a play at the Olivier Theatre and hardly noticed the revolving stage.

The play is translated by Christopher Hampton. I can't pretend to know whether it's faithful to the text, but I was crying at the end, from a mixture of elation, admiration and emotion. I clapped my hands so much they still hurt.

# Things We Do For Love

## Gielgud Theatre, August 1998

It's irrelevant and possibly impertinent of me to mention that Alan Ayckbourn is a great playwright; people far more qualified than myself have paid tribute to his theatrical brilliance and superb mastery of tragedy presented as comedy. Who can forget *Absurd Person Singular*, *The Norman Conquests* or *Just Between Ourselves*? He is also a great director who has managed, where so many others have failed, to keep a provincial repertory company not just alive but vibrantly kicking.

That said, I was disappointed with the acclaimed *Things We Do For Love*, now showing at the Gielgud Theatre. The action takes place in the house of Barbara, a career woman who has had sex only twice, once when she was at school – the boy had a nosebleed so we gather it was unsatisfactory – and the next time with her boss, who is married with children and a roving eye.

Nikki, a school-friend of Barbara's, arrives with her betrothed, Hamish, to rent Barbara's upstairs flat. At school, Nikki was a fourth-former when Barbara was head prefect. Barbara was then spiky, intelligent and honest, and Nikki had a crush on her; she still has. Barbara is still spiky and intelligent, but now she's repressed. On the face of it, poor dithering Nikki, with her period pains and her propensity for falling for men who beat her up, is in love with the seemingly gentle Hamish, though it's obvious she wants a daddy rather than a husband. I say seemingly because Hamish has recently walked out on his wife and children.

At first Hamish and Barbara hate each other, but within a matter of days they jump into bed and immediately discover that they are deeply in love. This strikes me as very unconvincing, since both of them are old enough to know better. They might feel a degree of fondness after a year or two, but 24 hours is going it a bit. Barbara does say he's got a 'big one', but then size is not supposed to be everything, and Barbara's hardly in a position to make comparisons.

The only character I did believe in was Gilbert, tenant of the downstairs flat, who has painted a naked picture of Barbara on his ceiling and is hoarding her old underwear thrown out for Oxfam. I would have preferred Barbara to have given Hamish the push and gone off with him. Actually, I've never seen underwear on display in Oxfam, though I do know plenty of chaps like Gilbert; perhaps that's because I live in Camden Town. I liked Nikki too; she was warm and vulnerable, and, apart from cutting up Hamish's trousers, went on her solitary way with great dignity.

I was alone, needless to say, in my non-appreciation of the play; the matinée audience about me fairly rolled in the aisles. Either most of them had only done it twice or else I'm world weary.

The cast were brilliant, though Barbara shrieked a bit and Hamish had a funny accent. Gilbert was bliss. He's that chap on the TV advert who, while in the loo, overhears his colleagues saying he's going to be made redundant, and comes out and croons, 'There may be trouble ahead, but while there's moonlight, and music, and love and romance . . . let's face the music and dance.' I'd dance with Gilbert any time, possibly with the aid of a zimmer frame.

# Oh! What a Lovely War

## Roundhouse, October 1998

Last week I went to the Roundhouse in Chalk Farm, London, to see *Oh! What a Lovely War*, that superb musical entertainment about the dreadful savagery of the First World War. I took with me my 4-year-old grandson, Inigo, who was beside himself at the prospect of seeing soldiers with guns.

Never having been inside the Roundhouse before, I was blown away, as they say, by its magnificence. Designed by George Stephenson, it was built in 1846 as an engineering maintenance and turning shed for steam engines. In future, I shall look upon the phrase 'the train glided into the station' in a new light. The residents living in the vicinity of Euston station objected to the smoke and noise of the trains and so the engines puff-puffed into Chalk Farm depot, were attached to a winch, turned round and pulled backwards into the station. Though a marvel of its age, it was only in use for 25 years, after which it was sold to Gilbey's to serve as a warehouse for gin. In 1964 it was nearly pulled down, and would have been but for the intervention of Arnold Wesker, who based his Centre 42 there.

For this particular production the space serving as the foyer – the cobblestones and marks of the rail track can still be seen – has been set about with hoop-la stalls, ice-cream stands and a rifle range. On the strict understanding that he would never tell his mother, Inigo had a go with a pop-gun, but his fingers were too small.

Joan Littlewood's original production was conceived as an end-of-the-pier entertainment, not just because Pierrots were particularly popular in 1914, but rather to underline the senseless honour of the trenches. The performance must never be allowed to become sentimental, however poignant and heart-stopping the songs of the period, only full of sentiment.

The storyline concerns war-games, the stupidity of the generals, the profiteering of the weapon manufacturers, the dogged persistence and fortitude of the ordinary soldiers and the ignorance of the public. And what songs! 'Roses of Picardy'; 'Keep the Home Fires Burning'; 'Hush Here Comes a Whizzbang'; 'They Were Only Playing Leapfrog'. On stage a handful of men die over and over again, only to spring upright for the next battle, the next chorus. In life, ten million men died trapped in a sea of mud stretching from the Alps to the English Channel.

The energy of the cast, which numbers about sixteen and seems double that, is phenomenal. It is impossible to single out one performance as better than another, though Rebecca Lock has a beautiful voice and David Ameil the drive and invention of a George Stephenson.

I'm now teaching Inigo to recite the last verse of 'In Flanders Fields' by John McCrae:

Take up our quarrel with the foe;
To you from falling hands we throw
The torch; be yours to hold it high.
If ye break faith with us who die
We shall not sleep, though poppies grow
In Flanders fields.

# Cleo, Camping, Emmanuelle and Dick

## National Theatre, December 1998

Full of enthusiasm after seeing *Cleo, Camping, Emmanuelle and Dick* at the National Theatre, I urged a young friend to buy tickets, to which she haughtily replied that the actors were merely doing impersonations of the original cast of the Carry On films. I did wonder what she thought any actor in any role was supposed to be doing, but held my tongue.

The first of the Carry On films was screened in 1958, the year which saw CND's first Aldermaston march and the opening night of Pinter's *The Birthday Party*; the last in the original series, *Carry On Emmanuelle*, appeared in 1978, the year in which Sid Vicious of The Sex Pistols died and the first test-tube baby was born.

Those of us who remember the films are familiar with the names of their leading actors – Barbara Windsor, Kenneth Williams, Sid James, Bernard Bresslaw, Joan Sims, Jim Dale, Peter Butterworth, Ken Connor, Charles Hawtrey and Hattie Jacques. Along the way Bob Monkhouse appeared – also, and rather astonishingly, Juliet Mills and Phil Silvers. According to Kenneth Williams's delicious diaries, the latter was a pain in the neck. In 1967 he took over the lead from Sid James, causing Williams to record, 'He's just terrible . . . so he's a worthy successor.'

The action of *Cleo, Camping, Emmanuelle and Dick* takes place in a 'happy camper' marooned in a field of mud during the filming of one or two of the Carry On films. I can't be more precise because these days theatre programmes don't feel it necessary to spell out where or when the action is taking place. Sometimes Barbara was in a wench's outfit and Williams in a Roman toga, and towards the end Sid

James wore a long skirt and what looked like an Elizabethan head piece.

Not that it mattered. The set was terrific, the actors, against wonderful backcloths of suburban pubs, catering buses and fields with the rain pelting down, approached the caravan with heads bent and feet encased in plastic bags.

The happy camper is for the comfort of Sid, much to the annoyance of Williams. Between them is an uneasy love/hate relationship (though in Williams's diaries the love bit is definitely missing). The bond between them is physical rather than emotional, as both suffer from extremely painful piles. Williams, especially, feels that the making of such films is beneath him, but it's obvious they afford him companionship – which, at this point in his career, is more important than an income, though he does his best to sabotage likeability by exposing himself and talking dirty whenever the opportunity arises.

The play is based on fact, and what an odd, complicated lot they were – Hawtrey permanently blotto, Sid madly in love with Barbara, Barbara standing by her Ronnie in prison, Williams torn to bits with self-loathing, and all of them living out chunks of their lives within the confines of a Carry On existence. And what about Imogen Hassall – I'd never heard of her – a dark bombshell who services Sid in his caravan and kills herself young?

Terry Johnson's play is marvellously well written, a feast of language superbly served up by a brilliant cast. OK, Barbara impersonates the walk, Williams the snigger, Sid the laugh, but not often. What remains is not a carry-off of a Carry On, but a brilliant exposition of character and a nostalgic glimpse of a past in which innuendo, once considered vulgar, is now infinitely more witty and closer to the truth than the present explicit interpretation of the sexual urge. This is real theatre and a must for a Christmas outing.

# 1999

Death of Iris Murdoch, Ernie Wise, Oliver Reed, Dirk Bogarde, Jennifer Patterson, Dusty Springfield and Alf Ramsey.

Gales and storms lash England and Europe.
Two million are without electricity.

The Dome opens.

Peter Mandelson back from the cold after nine months' exile.

*Good*, by C. P. Taylor, is about a man suffering from self-deception and moral inertia. It embodies Taylor's constant theme of the need for total integrity.

# Vassa

## Albery Theatre, March 1999

Recently I went to see *Vassa* by Maxim Gorky, currently showing at the Albery Theatre, St Martin's Lane. I rate highly both the acting of Sheila Hancock and the directorial magic of Howard Davies, but I had read a review which said something about it being not what Gorky had intended.

Apparently he wrote two versions, 20-odd years apart, the first featuring a strong woman who was prepared to commit murder and mayhem in order to keep her family together, the second portraying a mum doing much the same thing, but with love of money being the driving force. I don't know which version I saw, it being, in any case, an adaptation by Howard Davies, but as a novelist I am always astonished at the amazing powers, in regard to a writer's intentions, possessed by reviewers and critics. What I saw was a superbly crafted play, magnificently acted and directed, containing enough home truths to give us pause and send us home wounded.

Vassa has two sons and a daughter. We are in Russia round about 1911 – as with all programmes these days it is not felt necessary to tell one where or when the action is taking place. The set is huge and of great depth, with many doors. Upstairs, Vassa's husband lies dying, a state he's been in for some time. Pavel, her crippled son, has just returned from putting a cat in the pigeon house, mostly to annoy his Uncle Prokhor. Pavel's wife is missing from the marital bedroom, having spent the night with Prokhor. The factory, which has been Vassa's life's work, is in hock to Prokhor. As she knows that he has a dicky heart it is in everyone's interest that he should be provoked as much as possible. The children don't know about the debt. Once Dad upstairs has passed on they believe they will inherit. There not yet being a Welfare State, all three want the money so that they can get away from Mother.

On the surface, who can blame them? Vassa has benefited from murder, engaged in blackmail and encouraged the exploitation of her own daughter-in-law. For her, the ends justify the means; the family, however miserable, must stick together.

Gorky, poor fellow, had a terrible childhood and adolescence. His father died when he was three from cholera caught from Gorky. His mother married again and sent him off to live with a grandmother who beat him and who died when he was 11. At 12 he ran away and tramped all over Russia, working as a baker, a docker, a night watchman and a dish-washer on a Volga steamer. It was in this last job that he met a cook who encouraged him to read books. Wherever he went he was beaten and ill-used, and at 18 he attempted suicide, which left him with a damaged lung. Things got better for him later on, though he was frequently exiled for being too critical of events following the Revolution.

I found the character of Vassa extremely interesting, and have since wondered if Gorky put a lot of himself into her. She was very strong, for a woman, or do I mean single-minded?

The acting is exemplary, the set thrilling, the direction of the highest order. Several times I was forced to hiss 'You b——,' at yet another example of Vassa's cold manipulation.

# Good

I've always believed that painters, playwrights, novelists and actors can never leap much beyond the length of their own selves. If you look at the work of great portrait painters, the eyes always have the look of the artist, and it's surely the same with writers and thespians. Possibly it's the same with composers, but then I know nothing about music.

I never saw Alan Howard in the 1981 original production of C. P. Taylor's play Good, now revived at the Donmar Warehouse, but I've been told about it, and can well believe he gave a definitive performance as Halder, the academic persuaded to join the SS. I once wrote a television play in which he was cast as a weak vicar entangled in adultery and murder. It wasn't a very profound piece, indeed it was written as part of a melodramatic series, but Howard portrayed him with such brooding misery and introspection one could almost weep for him.

Charles Dance is now cast as Halder, and it's not that he isn't a fine actor, just that he's muscular, logical, persuasively normal. He's also very handsome, and there's the rub; in dealing with the Third Reich and the ethnic cleansing of the Jews one would prefer a maniac, and an ugly one at that, to be involved.

The plot, more or less, is as follows. Halder is a professor in Frankfurt living with a wife who can neither cook nor keep the house clean and a blind mother who is jolly aggressive. In the 1930s he publishes a book whose theme suggests that the insane, the deformed, might be better off dead – in other words, euthanasia is good. In that respect, when one thinks of the option of abortion in cases of

Down's Syndrome and other birth defects, the idea seems to have caught on.

Hitler reads Halder's book and dispatches officials to recruit him into the Nazi party. Chuffed, though not entirely convinced, Halder finally succumbs to flattery. As he assures his best friend – indeed his only friend – Maurice, who happens to be Jewish, Hitler is, after all, nothing more than a flash in the pan, and all this funny business about getting rid of Jews will soon be forgotten. Along the way Halder falls in love with a young student, beautifully and robustly played by Emilia Fox, leaves his wife and children, refuses to help Maurice to take flight to Switzerland and eventually fits himself into the enchanting uniform of an officer in the SS.

He is, of course, shown to be deluded. This is highlighted by his persistent hearing of melodies played by German bands. I liked the production of this very good play, particularly the use of gramophone records featuring Richard Tauber, who was himself accused of being a Nazi sympathizer. There is nothing more guaranteed to bring a lump to the throat than the great tenor's rendering of 'We Are In Love With You, My Heart And I'.

A month or so back a reader of this magazine chided me for not mentioning that *The Weir* contained four-letter words. In my defence I can only say I didn't notice them, possibly because they were spoken in an Irish brogue and, in any case, not delivered in anger. I did notice them in *Good*, particularly when Maurice was speaking, but then, he was contemplating a train ride to the gas ovens and Halder wasn't listening.

# The Gin Game

## Savoy Theatre, June 1999

I feel it my duty to warn all all *Oldie* readers, particularly those deficient in hearing and eyesight, not to waste their pension money buying stall seats at the Savoy Theatre. Far better to book into the gods or the circle, as the closer one gets to the stage the nearer one approaches the crust of the earth. It's all right going down, but coming up to the gents, the ladies or the street, oxygen is a necessity. Also, don't expect a cup of coffee in the interval or a pleasant smoke. Regulations list the first as unavailable and the second as prohibited, possibly because the theatre was destroyed by fire in 1990.

All the same, I can't think why there shouldn't be a room patrolled by the unemployed and homeless – plenty of whom are slumped outside in the Strand – armed with extinguishers to be used at the first curl of unbridled smoke. The enterprise could be paid for by tips from grateful patrons, either in money or in tins of dog food urgently needed by their numerous canine friends.

By a coincidence, *The Gin Game*, the drama now showing at the Savoy, directed by the great Firth Banbury and starring those two diamonds of the theatrical world, Joss Ackland as Weller and Dorothy Tutin as Fonsia, is also about rules and regulations. Housed in an American Old People's Welfare Home, the two and only characters are drawn together – and later torn apart – by the playing of a card game, gin rummy.

Weller is a fighter, on the surface, at least, raging against the dark and not likely to die nicely. Fonsia is proud, unhappy, and outwardly submissive. She doesn't like Weller swearing and she can't help winning every game that they play. She knows that it's all up with her, that age and death hold the last card. Weller, in spite of his roarings and determination to dig at the truth, is the weaker of the two.

The programme lists the triumphs of *The Gin Game*, the world-wide performances and the prizes it won for its author, D. L. Coburn, among them four Tony awards and a Pulitzer Prize. I must admit that I'm puzzled as to its success. It's almost a good play: the dialogue is real, the characters interesting – yet nothing really happens. One can't even class it as a period piece, a breakthrough of its kind: for me, 1977 happened yesterday. *Death of a Salesman* by Miller or Tennessee Williams's *Glass Menagerie* were far more gutsy, and their curtains fell on a climax. J. B. Priestley in his Time plays performed the same circular magic.

*The Gin Game* doesn't have an end, not really, beyond Weller getting finally beaten at cards and stumping off, outplayed for ever, into the hellish community room of the Welfare Home, leaving Fonsia centre stage. She just utters a little cry, 'Oooh,' or maybe, 'Oooh . . . noooh', and that's it. Perhaps to nudge the audience in the right direction, the programme prints a poem by Pushkin, the last few lines of which read:

> I know that I shall taste of happiness,
> Once more I shall be drunk on strains divine,
> Be moved to tears by musings that are mine;
> And haply when the last sad hour draws nigh,
> Love with a farewell smile may gild the sky.

Perhaps I've been too harsh. Whatever the content, the play is worth seeing for the performances of Tutin and Ackland. Now there's a taste of happiness.

# 2000

Death of Sir John Gielgud, Sir Alec Guinness, Douglas Fairbanks Jr, Hedy Lamarr, Jason Robards, and Barbara Cartland.

Dome useless says Duke of Edinburgh.

Betty Boothroyd to retire as Speaker of House of Commons.

*Cinderella* is obviously a glaring example of what is now regarded as a politically incorrect drama. The fact that her two sisters are prefixed by the adjective 'Ugly' is to be deplored.

# Cinderella

## Hackney Empire, February 2000

Did you know that our modern Aladdin is based on a burlesque written in the 1860s by H. J. Byron, who came up with the name Widow Twankey because clippers at the time were scudding home from the East with cargoes of something called 'twankay'? No, I've no idea either: perhaps an original version of sweet and sour! And were you aware that Bo-Peep and Little Boy Blue came from *Goody Two Shoes*, written by none other than Oliver Goldsmith? *Cinderella*, on the other hand, was devised partly from Perrault's short story *Les Fées* and partly from the plot of Rossini's unfairylike opera *La Cenerentola*, which featured the character Dandini. This is why, rather than being an offspring of Lord Smith, Cinders is always the daughter of a Baron and her wicked stepmother always a Countess.

Which brings me to the Hackney Empire and its production of a magnificent pantomime directed by Susie McKenna. Right from the first deafening opening bars of the orchestra, the audience joined in. What oohs of admiration arose as the Good Fairy came on, and rightly so, for she had a glorious voice and a presence that dominated the stage. What a fervent hissing broke out at the entrance of the wicked stepmother, dressed to kill in black satin.

The theatre was packed right up to the gods, and there were hundreds of children screaming with delight at an entertainment that encouraged their participation. One knew, by the way they roared with laughter, that their hatred of the Ugly Sisters was only assumed, just as one could tell they truly thought Cinderella was beautiful, even in her rags. My grandson, August, aged four, fell for her with a vengeance. He shouted out he wanted to marry her. Later, I was moved by his hold on reality, for though his lip trembled when she danced with Prince Charming, he applauded heartily when the glass slipper fitted and they danced off into the future. I think he realized he'd been born too late. Two hundred years ago this sort of emotional reaction was commonplace at Drury Lane, even if it was Garrick playing Hamlet. We've become awfully silent in the interim, awfully well behaved.

The Hackney Empire *Cinderella* stuck very closely to the original – love at first sight, a pumpkin turned into a carriage fit for a princess, the clock striking midnight. The Dome wasn't mentioned, or New Labour, and though there was nothing overtly suggestive in the way of dialogue, the Ugly Sisters were deliciously naughty and anarchic. The entire cast was dedicated, animated, enormously energetic.

The building needs refurbishment and is seeking funds; the gilt is peeling, the carpeting threadbare, the scenery still pulled up and down by ropes, something which was common in my youth and gave employment. None other than lovely Griff Rhys Jones is Chairman of the Appeal Committee, and one can trust him to ensure that the sweat, illusion and magic isn't swept away along with the antiquated plumbing.

If you miss this pantomime, Susie McKenna is back next Christmas directing *Mother Goose*. Remember to book early.

# The Family Reunion

## Barbican, April 2000

All of us from time to time are subjected to family reunions, many of which have considerable dramatic impact, though I have never been to one where the arguments are conducted in blank verse. T. S. Eliot's play, *The Family Reunion*, at present in repertory at the Barbican, is both powerful and extremely mysterious.

It is Amy, the Dowager Lady Monchensey's birthday, and she's expecting the arrival of her three sons to help blow out the candles. Waiting with her in the family home, Wishwood, are two elderly brothers of her dead husband, her three younger sisters, Ivy, Violet and Agatha, Dr Warburton, an old family friend, and Mary, daughter of a deceased cousin.

Something awful has happened to Amy in the past, which is why she's unable to give a straight answer to the most ordinary of questions. When one of the brothers-in-law asks her what time the boys are due to arrive, she replies: 'I do not want the clock to stop in the dark . . . I keep Wishwood alive, To keep the family alive, to keep them together, To keep me alive. . . . You none of you understand how old you are and Death will come to you as a mild surprise, A momentary shudder in a vacant room.'

Harry, the eldest and favourite son, following an unsuitable marriage, has been away for many years. Something awful has happened to him too, namely the death of his wife. It is believed that she was swept overboard during a storm at sea. However, when Harry arrives, he wastes little time on polite conversation and hastens to confess that he killed her: 'It was only reversing the senseless direction / For

161

a momentary rest on the burning wheel / That cloudless night in the mid-Atlantic / When I pushed her over.' He then talks about ghosts, about voices, which upsets his mother so much that she has to go and lie down. In the rest of Act I, Dr Warburton tries to tell him that his mother is not at all well, and Mary, who loves him, struggles to understand his state of mind.

Act II is rather surprising, for the way Harry's wife died is never referred to again, at least not in actual terms, and instead a police sergeant arrives with news that brother John has had a slight accident in fog and will be in hospital overnight. There's also a telephone call from brother Arthur who says he can't come up from London until tomorrow as he's without a car. The truth is, Arthur has been arrested for drunken driving – one could say they're a dysfunctional family.

At the arrival of the kindly sergeant I was reminded of J. B. Priestley's *An Inspector Calls*, in which a warning is given that sin begets sin and that justice must be done. So too in *The Family Reunion*, T. S. Eliot's masterly reworking of *Aeschylus' Eumenides*, with Harry as Orestes pursued by the Furies.

It might be thought that so abstract a work, and particularly one written in verse, would be difficult to appreciate, but that isn't the case. The play is both immediate and affecting, and somehow familiar, as if one's heard the words before, a long time ago. This underlines my belief that poetry should be learnt in schools as it used to be, line by line like a parrot, for then it is never forgotten.

The acting is a bit uneven, but Greg Hicks and Zoe Waites are excellent. What is difficult is to actually book to get in to see them. Nobody ever answers the box office telephone and the dates of performances listed in the newspapers are not always reliable.

# Baby Doll

## Albery Theatre, September 2000

When the film *Baby Doll* was released in 1956, Cardinal Speilman denounced it from the pulpit of St Patrick's Cathedral in New York City, proclaiming its theme to be a contemptuous defiance of natural law. He didn't say what he meant by this, but a review in *Time Magazine* did it for him – 'Just possibly the dirtiest American-made motion picture that has ever been legally exhibited . . .'.

I'd heard of the film, but in my ignorance I took it to be an adaptation of an original play by Tennessee Williams. It was not until I went to the Albery Theatre, where *Baby Doll* is now showing, and read Christopher Bigsby's excellent programme essay, that I understood the reverse was the case, and that what I was about to see was a further adaptation of the screenplay written by Elia Kazan, based on two one-act dramas penned by Tennessee Williams in 1940. Late in life, Williams wrote several drafts of a stage version of the film, entitled *Tiger Tail*. The director, Lucy Bailey, has woven together Kazan's film script and *Tiger Tail* and triumphantly come up with the present production of *Baby Doll*.

This preamble is important, because Bailey uses cinema techniques. For instance, the play starts with a close-up of a light in a window, and enlarges to show a girl lying in a cot. Then there is a fade-out and titles appear, plus the place and the date. Some scenes are played as if the camera is zooming in, others in 'long shot', both devices being extremely effective. The staging is simply stunning. There are no revolving platforms or any of that sort of mechanical trickery; it's all done by superb lighting and a brilliantly constructed set.

The place is Mississippi, that celluloid Deep South featuring happy Negroes singing on cotton plantations familiar to those of us who used to sit in the one-and-nines of yesterday. There's no singing in this Mississippi, and the Negroes know their place. There are four main characters: the pitiable Aunt Rose; the skinny, balding cotton grower, Archie Lee; Silva, the handsome Italian, manager of the Syndicate Plantation, and Baby Doll, a slender girl, so childish as to seem positively half-witted, who is married to Archie. The marriage has never been consummated, because Baby Doll isn't ready for that sort of thing, though there was a bargain struck that she would become a proper wife on her 20th birthday.

Archie, put out of business by the arrival of Silva and his more up-to-date production methods, burns down the Syndicate's cotton gin the night before the important date. Silva finds out and gets his subtle revenge. With the exception of Paul Brennen as the frustrated Archie, who understandably gets a little hot under the collar, no one takes their clothes off just to be provocative, or uses rude words. All the same, the play quivers throughout with unexpressed longings.

Charlotte Emmerson as Baby Doll is quite outstanding. She looks so innocent, and the way she can't quite run away from Silva is both touching and comic. Jonathan Cake as the clever, whip-wielding Silva is equally powerful. One almost believes he could love Baby Doll rather than use her. The amount of acting and directional talent produced by the drama schools and repertory companies of Britain never ceases to amaze.

# The Mystery of Charles Dickens

## Comedy Theatre, October 2000

In 1844 Charles Dickens wrote a letter to his biographer, Forster, which contained the following passage: 'I have often thought that I should certainly have been as successful on the boards as I have been between them. . . . I believed I had a strong perception of character and oddity, and a natural power of reproducing in my own person what I observed in others. . . . I practised immensely . . . often four, five, six hours a day.'

Some two or three years ago Peter Ackroyd also wrote a biography of Dickens; in parts, he brilliantly appeared to take on the personality of his subject rather than perform the function of a mere chronicler. *The Mystery of Charles Dickens*, now showing at the Comedy Theatre – alas, only for a limited run – is a scaled-down version of the book. The mystery of the title is a shade mysterious in itself, for, genius apart, Dickens seems to have suffered from the vicissitudes more or less common to all – his mother didn't understand him, his children and near relations died with regularity, his marriage grew stale, he became infatuated with a younger woman, he worked too hard and burned himself out.

Given that he was so gloriously addicted to performance and entertainment, to the magic of theatre and its grand illusions, it is perhaps surprising that Patrick Garland's otherwise excellent production is so lacking in visual excitement. I didn't see the point of the set, it being comprised of one upright gilt picture frame and a second one on its side.

Why couldn't we have had footlights, candles flaring, and a backcloth alive with images?

When it was said he lived in Bayham Street, Camden Town, a thoroughfare within walking distance of my own house, I longed to see a blown-up Victorian photograph of the time.

The curtain the audience saw on entering the auditorium was wonderful, a painting of Dickens sitting at the desk in his study surrounded by miniature images of the people he had created. Nudging the toe of his boot, little Nell lay dying. We might well have had that backcloth throughout; each time a book was mentioned the lights could have dimmed save on the one character to be portrayed. The sound of violins would have been welcome – to underline the pathos. It's true, as far as I know, that Dickens didn't go in for that sort of thing in his readings, but he pulled out all the stops in the Christmas entertainments he put on for his friends.

As it happens, this extra gilt on the gingerbread didn't matter, for the performance of Simon Callow as Dickens, or rather his portrayal of the characters he invented, is beyond criticism. Years ago I remember seeing Emlyn Williams doing the same thing, but he was too formal, too careful, less of a comedian. He was good, but it seemed to me he was pretending he wasn't an actor. Callow lets rip. He shows off, as Dickens did; he flaunts his theatricality; he has the rubber face, the sonorous voice and the loose limbs of the great exponents of the music hall. All over England and America, Dickens's reading of the bludgeoning to death of Nancy by Bill Sykes caused uproar. Women fainted and strong men groaned. This didn't quite happen at the Comedy, but Callow came devilishly close to generating horror.

# Copenhagen

## Duchess Theatre, November 2000

*Copenhagen*, the play by Michael Frayn now running at the Duchess Theatre, is not easy to review, its subject being so scientific and its time sequence so jumpy. It says everything for the skill of the playwright that in spite of such difficulties one's attention is held throughout. Perhaps it is helped by the somewhat static direction: save for sitting now and then on three chairs, the players just walk round and round the stage, which means there is little visual distraction and one can concentrate on the text.

The play opens with two ghosts, the Danish scientist Niels Bohr and his wife, Margrethe, waiting for the arrival in Copenhagen in 1941 of a third spirit, Werner Heisenberg. Bohr was the father of modern atomic physics, in that he realized as early as 1913 that quantum theory applied to matter as well as to energy. Heisenberg was first his student, then the son he might have wished for, then the inventor of quantum mechanics and the uncertainty principle. Unfortunately, he was also a German, and to visit an occupied country meant he had been given permission by the Nazis. The question of why and to what ends, and which side either scientist was on, lies at the heart of this morality play.

I imagine the characters of the two men are based on fact, whereas that of Margrethe is more imaginary, her input being necessary to voice what would remain unsaid were she not there. For instance, discussing the reason for the visit, she asks Bohr if it could have something to do with the war and the work on nuclear fission, to which he replies, 'Heisenberg is a theoretical physicist. I don't think anyone has yet discovered a way to use theoretical physics to kill people.'

Heisenberg's visit was real; the reasons behind it, in historic terms, still remain unclear. My understanding of it, at the end of the play, was that Heisenberg, far from wanting to steal fission secrets from Bohr, was requiring to be told by his mentor that the pursuit of science was an end in itself, and if weapons of destruction resulted, why, that was down to the uncertainty principle inherent in the make-up of man.

It seems to me that Heisenberg, as portrayed by Frayn, deliberately delayed discovering nuclear fission until the war was lost. Two years later, in August, the Allied scientists, Bohr among them, perfected the atomic bomb and we tested it out on Japan. So who was the more guilty, Heisenberg or Bohr?

It's Margrethe who has more or less the last word. She says, 'And when all our eyes are closed ... what will be left of our beloved world? Our beloved and mined world?' It is bleak to think that the dust once rising above Hiroshima is now largely forgotten.

When one goes regularly to the theatre, the content of many plays often leaks out overnight. One remembers the storyline, the acting, etc., but not the impact. This play remains with me. Perhaps one needs to have grown up during the Cold War to be affected by a dramatic discourse on nuclear fission.

Aeons ago, there was an upset in the world called the Bay of Pigs. Kennedy was involved, and so was I. For the sole reason that I had a child in arms and another on the way, I was picked to go to the American consulate in Liverpool to protest against the threatened outbreak of nuclear war. Clutching my babe, I went, and was so overcome by the sight of a consul who resembled Gregory Peck that

I became tongue-tied. He was so charming – I was in the middle of becoming a single mother – that I forgot all about bombs. Now there's an example of the uncertainty principle.

# Notre-Dame de Paris

## Dominion Theatre, December 2000

In the past year it has become more and more difficult to write reviews of West End plays, particularly if the piece is intended for a monthly magazine. Either a new play is good – *To the Green Fields Beyond* – in which case it's booked out, or else it has a limited run and is over by the time *The Oldie* appears. Four National Theatre productions, *Hamlet*, *In Extremis*, *De Profundis* and *Peer Gynt*, all end before Christmas, as do *The Duchess of Malfi* and *The Tempest* at the Barbican, and *A Doll's House* at the New Ambassadors. Should you want, for old times' sake, to see a staging of the Noel Coward classic, *Brief Encounter*, you can't: it came off in November.

In despair, I settled for *Notre-Dame de Paris*, now showing at the Dominion Theatre, Tottenham Court Road. Though a gale was blowing and the rain descending in torrents, the huge theatre had an equally huge matinée audience, something which, in my experience, does not always bode well.

*Notre-Dame de Paris*, better known as *The Hunchback of Notre-Dame*, is based on the novel by Victor Hugo, of whose dramatic works it was said that they were 'masterpieces in all but their fitness for the stage'. The words 'based on', in the context of this musical, are misleading; 'skimmed off' would be more accurate. The story is told entirely in what nowadays passes for song, so it's not easy to follow, not unless the Hunchback is on stage leering at the gypsy girl, Esmeralda, because then you know you ought to feel sad, he being so deformed and unlikely to win her love.

It's interesting the way songs are now constructed: first there are four lines spoken more or less on one note, followed by another sliding upwards and ending in a prolonged and deafening shout. Example: 'You are lying there / I see you lying there! You do not look at me / I who love you . . . / YOUR LOVE WILL KILL ME.'

I kept thinking of a description I'd read of how the theatrical gestures and articulation used by actors of a bygone generation, Kean and Irving and Garrick, if used today would cause a modern audience to fall about laughing. I suppose every age has its own style, and no doubt a pre-20th-century audience would find today's performers equally comical.

There are many good things in this production, including the wonderful sets, the lighting, the inspired acrobats and the dance routines. There is a 50-foot silver wall at the back of the stage studded with grappling irons, up which the dancers slither like so many lizards. Quasimodo comes from the flies upside-down inside a gigantic bell. Frollo, the naughty priest, played by Fred Johanson, has a magnificent voice. Alas, his is the only one, and unfortunately there isn't a decent song from first to last, which is a bit of a drawback in a musical, though it didn't stop those around me cheering and whooping their appreciation.

If you do go and see it, there is no need to take hearing aids, as the sound is amplified fit to burst eardrums.

One tip: buy a £10 seat in the stalls and move to the front when the lights go down.

# 2001

Death of Jack Lemmon, Nigel Hawthorne, Michael Williams, Anthony Quinn and George Harrison.

Tate Modern Turner Prize awarded to a piece entitled 'The lights going on and off'. That's all they did.

Jeffrey Archer sentenced to four years' imprisonment on two counts of perverting the course of justice.

*Over the Top* is a play performed by my grandchildren in a back yard in Camden Town.

# Fallen Angels

## Apollo Theatre, January 2001

Noel Coward wrote two plays in 1923 – *The Vortex* and *Fallen Angels* – the former featuring a depraved mother and her drug-abusing son, the latter concerning two wives who, anticipating the arrival of a mutual lover from the past, drink themselves under the table. Both plays caused something of a scandal at the time, and *Fallen Angels* was nearly refused a licence on the grounds that the wives were portrayed as too rampantly eager to commit adultery. In 1958, Coward updated the play from the Twenties to the Thirties, a version now playing at the Apollo Theatre in Shaftesbury Avenue and starring Felicity Kendal and Frances de la Tour.

I didn't really think I'd enjoy it, not having seen a Coward play before and suspecting that it would be all clipped vowels and terribly, terribly smart one-liners. I also felt its characters would be spoilt, empty-headed and snobbish, and that, possibly owing to the brainwashing effects of political correctness, one would feel uncomfortable watching a light comedy set in a time when unemployment was rife and England was racing towards war. How wrong I was.

Julia (Felicity Kendal) has been friends with Jane (Frances de la Tour) since childhood. Of the two, Jane is the more impulsive, the more willing to chuck her bonnet over the windmill. Her husband, Wiffie (Eric Carte), is less gullible than Fred (James Wooley), or perhaps I mean less thick. Julia is terribly pretty, Jane something of a tomboy. Both, years before, though not at the same time, had an affair with Maurice, a devastating Frenchman wandering around Italy. Julia got him first, but lost him at the railway station in Pisa after some argument over a slice of sausage.

The only moment of doubt I experienced throughout the entire play, in regard to reality, was some few seconds after Jane entered with the news that Maurice was about to arrive, a doubt raised not so much by the nervous excitement exhibited by both women but rather from the amount of space they had in which to show it. Julia's living room was enormous; they couldn't have rampaged around with such freedom in an ordinary flat. That, and the fact that in spite of being married for a decade, neither woman appeared to have produced children. Either, I reasoned, they were both infertile, or more probably it was term-time and their offspring were lodged in a maximum security boarding school.

The drink taking hold – on stage, that is – I was hooked. There is not a dud line in the whole play, and in the interval arguments raged as to who was the best actress for delivery, timing and sincerity. Too difficult, and both Kendal and de la Tour are brilliantly served by Coward and Michael Rudman, the director. There's also a wonderful maid (Tilly Saunders) who plays the piano and sings divinely, and the lounge lizard, Maurice (Stephen Greif), whose final arrival was utterly convincing as to his ability to seduce. If you want to go to the theatre for a post-Christmas outing, go to this. It's such a relief to laugh out loud. *Fallen Angels* is terribly, terribly funny.

# The Accused

## Haymarket Theatre, February 2001

I once played a small part in a courtroom drama, and the curious thing was that the moment I climbed into the dock I became stiff as a ramrod. I can't remember what the play was called or anything about the plot, only that I wore a hat. I knew it wasn't a real courtroom – the audience were energetically rattling their interval teacups – but still I had the curious notion it would be fatal to give any sign of being alive.

This recollection came back to me last month when, at the Haymarket Theatre, the curtain rose – or rather, part of the stage lit up – on Jeffrey Archer's *The Accused*. There was a door marked 'Jury Room' at the front, and a clock on the wall telling the time: 9.45 am. As the house lights went down the door opened and the Jury Bailiff entered and told us the nature of the charge, the name of the accused, and who would defend and who would prosecute. Then the door lifted and we were in the courtroom of the Old Bailey, with the Judge in his crimson robes seated in a sort of organ loft high up on the wall.

Mr Patrick Sherwood, senior consultant and head of the Cardiothoracic Unit of St George's Hospital, was to be tried for the murder, by poison, of his wife. The chief witness for the prosecution was a nurse who had worked in the same unit at St George's and who gave damning evidence of his culpability. He had courted her, driven her home in his car, taken her to the theatre, slept with her and promised to marry her. Then he'd dropped her. He did not get on with his wife and had fairly recently taken out a joint life insurance policy. The nurse could prove he'd been intimate with her, because he had a small burn on his arm, though that, of course, she might have seen when he scrubbed up in the hospital.

The prosecution were out to brand her as a woman scorned and one acting out of pique, but I rather liked her. She was at least giving the impression of being alive and upset, unlike Mr Sherwood, who gazed straight ahead and barely blinked – but then I believe the awful Dr Shipman behaved in a similarly impassive manner.

When Mr Sherwood, alias the author, Jeffrey Archer, was at last called to the witness box, the evidence against him was very flimsy. For one thing, he could never have taken the nurse home as she said because he couldn't drive and never had. And there was a riveting moment when he took off his shirt, turned his back to the audience and exposed an enormous burn mark across his spine, an injury sustained in Mrs Thatcher's war over the Falklands.

The summing up concluded, we, the audience, were asked to give our verdict as to whether he was guilty or not by pressing the little button in front of our seat. I thought this a shade suspect – who's to know the votes were counted correctly? The afternoon I went, the verdict was 'innocent', after which Sherwood told the nurse he was delighted they'd got away with it, but that he had no intention of marrying her after all.

What can one say, other that in parts the plot was rather good, the set terrific and some of the acting adequate? Beyond that the play was without depth and lacking in real characters, not least Sherwood, who came over as slick, heartless and far too cocky for his own good. I blame the parents . . . and the newspapers.

# Under the Doctor

## Comedy Theatre, April 2001

In the 1952 *Oxford Companion to the Theatre*, a farce is defined as an extreme form of comedy in which laughter is raised at the expense of probability, particularly by horse-play and bodily assault. Its subject is the inherent stupidity of man at odds with his environment, which could apply to most plays, intentionally funny or not.

I can just about remember appearing on telly – in the days when actors had to stand cheek by jowl because there was only one camera – in *Rookery Nook*, a farce by Ben Travers. I think that Peter Cushing played one of the leads. The only line I can remember, not mine, was 'Flags for the lifeboat, anyone?', delivered by Anona Wynn wearing frilly knickers and not much else.

Which brings me to Peter Tilbury's *Under the Doctor*, now showing at the Comedy Theatre, with Anton Rodgers and Peter Davison, both in splendid form, appearing in the main parts. The setting is Paris in 1912, possibly because of the Moulin Rouge and those underpants tied with a ribbon at the crotch worn by cancan dancers. At any rate, the ribbon is several times released from its bow, enabling the doctor to pleasure himself.

The plot is not easily explained, there being so many twists, turns and misunderstandings, which is as it should be. Sufficient to say that the doctor, Davison, has been a naughty boy with a lady patient, the one with the cancan drawers, and to allay the suspicions of his wife has had to think up an excuse as to where he's been all night. This one excuse – attending to a dying male patient – gets him out of the frying-pan and into a series of bigger and more furiously burning fires. He is aided and abetted by his manservant Etienne, alias Anton Rodgers, who does very well out of such deceptions, being handed 500 francs for every dilemma he momentarily solves.

Unfortunately, the male patient, Bassinet, robustly played by Robert Swann, refuses to act the dying man, and has to be chloroformed, and worse, to keep him quiet. A rare piece of medical equipment is sent for, a gloriously Heath Robinson contraption hurriedly assembled by the downstairs caretaker, which is passed off to some as an ultra-modern heart machine and to others as a sculpture by Picasso.

The involved relationships multiply. The awkward patient who refuses to act as though dying is the lover of the doctor's mother-in-law. The husband of the lady patient with the beribboned knickers is about to be the lover of the doctor's wife, mainly because Etienne, for the best of motives, has explained that the doctor can no longer get it up and would welcome attention paid to her on medical grounds.

The funny thing about farce is that it needs participation. There's an advert on the telly at the moment, set in a barber's shop, in which a customer starts laughing when his neck is tickled with the brush. The shop is full, and everyone starts laughing. I was at the matinée of *Under the Doctor* and unfortunately the audience was sparse. I did laugh, but had there been more people I would have laughed more.

# *Lulu*

## Almeida Theatre, May 2001

When I was in my teens someone showed me a black-and-white photograph of a girl with a pouting mouth and what used to be called an evacuee haircut. She was, so I was told, a cinema star called Louise Brooks, who had appeared as the lead in a foreign film of 1928 entitled *Die Buchse der Pandora* – Pandora's Box. I must have known something more about this film because, 40 years later, when writing a novel about a girl starting out on a career in the theatre, I conceived of her as being so innocent, yet so knowing, that she might have been considered simple. The play, *Lulu*, is now showing at the Almeida Theatre, Kings Cross. The old Almeida is being 'refurbished', and the company's temporary home is a converted bus depot. I thought the surroundings splendid, not least the naughty video shop on the corner.

*Lulu* was written by Frank Wedekind in 1892, which comes as a surprise, for the play is a very modern tragedy. It was never performed in his own lifetime in the way that he had intended, for obvious reasons – even now it is immensely dark and disturbing. Determined to see it performed, Wedekind hacked it to pieces, and finally split it in half and made two separate plays, *Earth Spirit* and *Pandora's Box*. Neither piece had the power of the original, but both caused enough of a sensation to inspire Berg's great opera and five silent films.

It is the story of a young girl who uses men and is used in return, and who displays no rage, terror or shock at the way she is treated. Nor does she show anything but a fleeting sadness when those men she has professed to love die violently or pass from her life. She is never angry with anybody, or surprised by their behaviour; she is simply a beautiful creature ready to be mounted by all who show interest. Sometimes she doesn't have to be paid. When betrayed or left she smiles and turns to the next encounter.

There were many arguments in the interval about Lulu. Some thought her merely a sex-crazed animal, others that she was out for money and power and enjoyed seeing men suffer. I thought she was an innocent, and behaved as she did because it was expected of her and she liked to please. From the age of five she'd been abused by her revolting brute of a father and sold on to various men with money and position. Nothing really upsets her; she does as she's told and remains incorruptible.

The part of Lulu must have been very difficult to cast. She has to be able to act and to look right without clothes, two things which don't often go together. I dislike nudity on stage and find it both off-putting and boring, but Anna Friel is quite amazing. No matter how little she wears or how often she opens her legs she is never less than pleasing to look upon, and her grace of movement makes her antics seem natural rather than salacious. Alan Howard in the part of the world-weary Dr Schoning is equally real. One feels that for all his cynicism he really did love Lulu.

This is not an easy play to review in a short space, it being both profound and magical. There are certain dramatic pieces, *Richard II*, *Death of a Salesman*, *Hamlet*, *Johnson Over Jordan*, in which the main character is the play. *Lulu* belongs in the same category.

# A Midsummer Night's Dream

## Albery Theatre, June 2001

I would travel many miles, possibly on foot, to watch Derek Jacobi on stage, and the odd mile further if he was appearing in a play by Hugh Whitemore. Last week I walked perhaps half a mile to see him on the stage of the Vaudeville Theatre in Whitemore's *God Alone Knows*, only to be informed at the box office that the matinée had been cancelled. Flustered, I wandered in various directions and presently found myself facing the Albery Theatre adorned with billboards advertising *A Midsummer Night's Dream*.

This is not a dramatic piece I would have rushed towards were it not for a brief encounter with a reader of *The Oldie* at the last Simpson's luncheon who said he liked my reviews because I was never nasty. This did not please me as much as it should, for it implies a certain lack of backbone. It is true that I find it hard to rubbish a play, mostly because I'm only too aware of the money, hard work and high hopes that accompany such a venture, which was why I promptly bought a ticket for the *Dream* on the grounds that I could say what I liked about Will Shakespeare without causing offence.

The last time I saw the play was in the Park and it rained, and the time before that in a production at the National in which the actors were up to the buttocks in mud and the first three rows of the stalls had to wear protective clothing. The reasoning behind such a mud-bath was explained in the programme: at the time Will wrote his play the area around Stratford was apparently under water from a great storm. Both productions were charming, received reverentially and accompanied by the sound of sloshing.

On first taking my seat at the Albery I thought the play had already begun; there were people wandering about the stage to the music of Larry Clinton and his orchestra. Bottom was folding sheets, watched by Lysander and Demetrius wearing the uniforms of the army and the RAF. Several cleaning ladies in turbans were having a gossip. The set was empty save for a huge fireplace in the middle with a mirror above it. Hundreds of schoolchildren making a din fell silent as the house lights dimmed.

For those very few who do not know the play, the title says it all. Most of the action takes place at night and most of the characters are forever falling asleep and dreaming. A stern father wants his daughter, Hernia, to many Demetrius who is loved by Helena. Hermia loves Lysander and the two arrange to meet in woods inhabited by fairies, where a group of rustics led by Bottom happen to be rehearsing a play to be performed before the Court.

I have the impression that in other productions I was waiting for the arrival of Bottom, but with Dawn French in the part he seemed to be there from the word go. This Bottom has the egotism of a confident child who loves showing off, and the comic truth of the performance appears to have infected the entire cast. From the moment the aeroplanes drone overhead and a huge explosion shatters the fireplace and the mirror to reveal the forest, we are deeply into the dream and can all believe in fairies.

This is a wonderful production, and no, I'm not just trying to be nice.

# Nixon's Nixon

## Comedy Theatre, September 2001

The West End theatre is in a bad way, not so much in regard to what is on show, but rather as to its accessibility. Time was when those interested in the drama could travel in from the suburbs by train or by car and spend an interesting evening sampling what was on offer. The bright lights illuminating the hoardings sparkled above well swept streets. No longer – the West End is now a dangerous country, empty of taxis, without parking facilities, its thoroughfares thronged with people who don't seem normal. One could grow roots waiting for a bus, which is why I go to matinées, and even then I often have to walk home.

That being said, visiting the Comedy Theatre to see *Nixon's Nixon* was worth the hassle. It didn't exactly come under the heading of a light-hearted afternoon, but in my book that's all to the good, seeing nowadays we get nothing but froth by way of entertainment from both newspapers and television. Time, running out as it is for some of us, should not be squandered.

Nixon must have had the same thoughts for, in March 1973, Gordon Liddy was convicted of conspiring to spy on the Democratic Party headquarters in the Watergate Building. A year later the House of Representatives Judiciary Committee handed down three articles of impeachment against Nixon – abuse of Presidential power, obstruction of justice and contempt of Congress. At eight o'clock on the evening of the 8th August, he summoned his Secretary of State, Henry Kissinger, to the Lincoln Room of the White House and remained closeted with him until midnight. The next morning he resigned.

Russell Lee's play – mistakenly advertised as a comedy – imaginatively deals with the three hours the two men spent together. What a terrible exposé of two men in charge of the world! What pitiful little pygmies, what egotistical, puffed-up examples of the human race! Nixon, who ordered massive bombing strikes against Hanoi, sheds tears at the thought of the loyalty shown him by his dog, Checkers. As the drink flows and he comes up with more and more outlandish plots to divert world attention from his predicament, he becomes a shade less detestable, for he's now a man apparently suffering physical as well as mental torture, and hobbles about the stage as though treading on hot coals. Maybe he had a bad back. Kissinger, he who laughably took home a Nobel Peace prize, plays his stooge, acting the part of Brezhnev and Chairman Mao; he's very good as the latter. He appears to humour his President but his eyes are watchful, his posture unyielding. Though he too is gulping down the whisky, he's a man keeping a sharp eye on his place in the lifeboat. Of the two I thought him the more culpable, but that's possibly because he didn't get as drunk.

There's no interval, but the play didn't seem too long. The ending is extremely exciting. As Nixon crazily outlines a mad plan to start another war and then step in as the peacemaker, the theatre is filled with the thunderous sound of an approaching chopper. Keith Jochim as Nixon and Tim Donoghue as Kissinger were excellent; both actors and play deserve larger audiences.

# *Caught in the Net*

## Vaudeville Theatre, October 2001

The plot of Ray Cooney's new farce, now showing at the Vaudeville Theatre, concerns a man who has two families, neither of whom knows of the existence of the other. The plot is not as far-fetched as it might seem. I know of two people, one being J. R. Ackerley, literary editor and author of *My Dog Tulip*, the other the late dear and greatly missed actor, David Tomlinson, who found their fathers had managed just such a deception. David's account of his dad glimpsed from the top of a bus, sitting up in bed accepting a cup of tea from a strange woman, is the very stuff of farce. Cooney's version of such a dilemma is more up to date, and involves the Internet. Not surprisingly, the title of the play is *Caught in the Net*, though I didn't catch on to its relevance until someone told me.

There were two things that struck me as not quite right about this new farce: one, the chap with the two families is a taxi-driver; and two, his children are very obedient. All the farces I've ever seen have centred round the upper classes, who mostly carry tennis rackets and often exit and enter through French windows. Their offspring, moreover, usually adopt a somewhat casual attitude when dealing with Papa.

That being said, *Caught in the Net* does have its moments, and the arrival of Eric Sykes, complete with zimmer frame, is one of them. Eric plays the Dad of Stanley, the put-upon lodger in the house of the taxi-driver. Russ Abbot as Stanley is very good indeed, almost as good as Eric, whose uncertain gait and manic smile had the audience roaring. It's not that the rest of the cast isn't splendid too, just that

Sykes is in command from the moment he enters, and Abbot, whose mouth and body seem to be made of india-rubber, has the best lines. It was he, somewhere towards the end of the first act, who eventually made me cry with laughter. To explain this, one can't do better than to quote John Lahr on the subject of farce. 'Farce', he wrote, 'is ruled by the law of momentum: at a certain speed, all things disintegrate. At speed panic substitutes for reason, and characters are pushed beyond guilt and beyond their connection to each other. The joke at the heart of farce mayhem is that people state their needs but the other characters, in their spectacular self-absorption, don't listen.'

The speed at which this particular farce progresses is indeed monumental. Wives and children are locked in rooms, mobile phones constantly ring and Eric is fairly flung up the stairs to get him out of sight. With the taxi-driver endlessly rushing between his two households to avert a confrontation – having become acquainted with each other on the Internet, the son of one family is hell-bent on meeting the daughter of the second – it is left to Stanley to keep them apart.

I don't know that this is one of Cooney's greatest successes, but the audience at the matinée seemed to love it, the mirth growing in volume and the applause heartfelt. I had a touch of sciatica in one leg that afternoon, and after I'd laughed it went away. Perhaps one shouldn't ask for more.

# Antarctica

## Savoy Theatre, November 2001

On 25 January 1911 Captain Robert Scott, at his winter quarters at Cape Evans, wished godspeed to six men setting off on a geographical survey of King Edward's Land to the North. The *Terra Nova* would deposit them in the region of Robertson Bay, and they should not expect the ship's return until the following winter. While they were away, Scott and his party would set off to conquer the South Pole. There would be difficulties, of course, but with God's help they would all meet up again the following year.

The six men were Lieutenant Campbell of the Royal Navy, his Petty Officers Abbott and Browning, Seaman Dickason, Surgeon Levick and the geologist Raymond Priestley. Scott and his party froze to death, Campbell's survived, but only just. David Young's ambitious new play, *Antarctica*, now at the Savoy Theatre, tells the story of the latter expedition.

The staging is imaginative – a huge movable sheet of glittering ice that can rise or fall or remain at an angle, so that the actors can climb out and appear as if on a ridge beneath the stars; to one side the corner of a cosy room in which the geologist Priestley sits reading from the expedition diary he kept so many years before.

I term this play ambitious because it is long, full of stories and myths, and endeavours to show us a world that is both real and imaginary. As the weather worsened and their food supplies dwindled – the ship failed to return for them – the men were reduced to rations consisting of one sugar cube, six raisins and a piece of chocolate. If they were lucky, they might venture out to kill seals, whose meat gave them enteritis. When their paraffin stocks were gone, they used blubber to burn in the stove, and its noxious fumes all but asphyxiated them. As they rotted, marooned in their inadequate shelter, each began to display signs of madness. Campbell was in charge, or thought he was, and wielded discipline as though head boy of a public school; Dickason was the noble, simple seaman, doing what he was told, content to take orders. Abbott became a thorn in the flesh, raging about poverty and revolution; he bit off the tip of his own finger when it rotted on his hand.

I found the most interesting character to be that of Levick, who more and more grew deafened by the thoughts in his head. It is he who questions whether the mind, rather than losing control under such conditions, begins to function as it was meant to.

This is not an easy play to watch. It requires concentration and a knowledge of 20th-century exploration. It should also be brutally cut, possibly by three quarters of an hour. The ending, when the expedition at last reaches safety, is abrupt and magical. The long winter darkness ends and a scarlet glow spreads across the backcloth.

When Scott's body was found, his diary was gripped under his arm. In it he had written these last words: 'Had we lived, I should have had a tale to tell of the hardihood, endurance and courage of my companions which would have stirred the heart of every Englishman.' *Antarctica*, the play, is just such another story.

# Over the Top

## December 2001

The inevitable side-effect of reviewing plays on a regular basis over a period of years, unless one is Kenneth Tynan, is an unfortunate blunting of excitement and wonder. For the last three decades so much money has been spent on visual effects – revolving stages, breathtaking sets and computer-operated lighting – that the drama itself has become all but buried.

I am thinking in particular of J. B. Priestley's *An Inspector Calls*, an updated production which has won every theatrical award and is still attracting capacity audiences. In my humble opinion, this modern version distorts and snuffs out, by virtue of its complicated staging, the original concept of the author. Plays should be about words, not sets or backcloths.

Which is why, last month, my faith in the enduring magic of the theatre was restored by a visit to an open-air production of *Over the Top*, performed by the Albert Street Players. I have to admit the historical accuracy of the play was open to question: it began with a spotlight on Churchill reciting his famous speech encouraging us to 'fight them on the beaches' etc., followed by the singing of 'Goodbye Piccadilly' and 'Pack Up Your Troubles in Your Old Kit Bag'. After that, the lights lowered, came up again, and we were in the trenches of the First World War. On stage stood a captain, a soldier and two nurses. The captain bellowed, 'I don't want to go over the top.' The nurses pointed at him and said, 'He doesn't want to go over the top.' The soldier said, 'I'd rather go to bed.'

Then the captain rang HQ and asked if it was possible

they could just stay in their trench. It wasn't, and while they waited for the dreadful moment they remembered poems. The youngest nurse went first. With great feeling she recited something along the lines of 'I like mice . . . they are nice.' The second nurse, beautifully played by Esmé G Davies, recalled a quaint old town and the fluttering hand-kerchiefs of yesterday. The men spoke of death:

> He turned towards me and I said,
> I am one of those who went before you
> Five and twenty years ago; one of the many who never
>     returned,
> One of many who returned and yet were dead.

In Act II the phone rang. They must climb out of the trenches in five minutes and face the enemy. They all kissed. The soldier, played by August Ford, said to the first nurse, Florence G Davies, 'Farewell, I leave my heart behind.' The captain, played by Inigo Ford, said to the second nurse, 'And mine with you.' The first nurse, turning to the audience, cried out, 'Mine is in bits.' Then, to suit-able music, the lads went over the top, first in slow motion, then headlong.

The performance took place in Camden Town on 3 November, two nights before a remembrance of Guy Fawkes, and as the actors leapt into the darkness three rockets went up and sprayed the night with stars. That wasn't the end. The dead soldiers rose from the imagined mud and blood and lined up with the weeping nurses; then cast and audience, voices punctuated by explosions, sang Rolf Harris's immortal song, 'Two Little Boys', the chorus of which begins: 'Did you think I would leave you dy-y-ying, when there's room on my horse for two'.

The acting was heartfelt, the staging minimal, the words memorable, but I doubt if this production will be transferred to the West End, not after that business in New York. Now that history counts for nothing, how can ten million slain in the mud of Flanders stand comparison with the three thousand buried beneath the rubble of the Twin Towers?

# 2002

Death of Dudley Moore, Linda Lovelace, Rod Steiger,
John Thaw, Spike Milligan and HRH the Queen Mum.

Rowan Williams succeeds John Carey as
Archbishop of Canterbury.

Collapse of trial of Paul Burrell for theft.

The play *Dr Johnson and Mrs Thrale* was enacted by myself,
Richard Ingrams and Raymond Banning. The review was
a ludicrous attempt to persuade the reader
I was someone else.

# Blood Brothers

## Phoenix Theatre, March 2002

In the sixties Liverpool became known all over the world as the home of the Mersey Beat. This was an undoubted triumph for those directly involved, but 40 years on this once great city – home in my youth of the most notable repertory company in England, of the Philharmonic Orchestra under Flash Harry, of the Sandon Studio Society and the most prestigious medical faculty in the country – remains shackled to the memory of the Beatles. It is now bidding to become the cultural centre of Europe, or is it the world? In order to gain this important title a list has been drawn up detailing some recent major 'cultural' achievements, among them World Capital of Pop in the *Guinness Book of Records*; the winning of three FC cups in one season; Michael Owen, Footballer of the Year: the grand opening of the new terminal at the John Lennon airport.

No mention is made of the Liverpool poets Adrian Henry, Roger McGough and Brian Patten, nor of the remarkable playwright Alan Bleasdale or the equally brilliant Willie Russell whose musical *Blood Brothers*, first produced in 1988, is still wowing audiences at the Phoenix Theatre in Charing Cross Road.

I first went to see the show eight years ago, and failed to appreciate it. I think I was still thinking of musicals in terms of *Guys and Dolls* and *Oklahoma*, whose songs were more memorable than the storyline. Seeing *Blood Brothers* for the second time recently, I now realize that I ought to have thought of the music as a moving accompaniment to a very dark and affecting drama.

The story is of a Liverpool girl and boy who go out

dancing, marry and have kids. Dad finally leaves, and single mum Mrs Johnstone finds herself pregnant with twins. The woman she cleans for is unable to bear children and begs her to give up one of them. The two boys, unaware of their kinship, meet and become friends. Mickey is poor, boisterous, full of life and largely uneducated. Eddie is sensitive, clever and a product of the public school system. There are scenes of enormous vitality in which Mickey and his gang, joined by the admiring Eddie, play their back-street games. The friendship can't last, of course; in adulthood the differences in their circumstances become too great. Eddie has a decent, well-paid job; Mickey spends time in prison and returns destroyed.

There are three outstanding performances in an excellent cast, those of Linda Nolan as Mrs Johnstone, Paul Crosby as Mickey and David Bingham as Eddie, the latter understudy to the actor Andrew Langtree. Linda Nolan is an utterly convincing warm-hearted Mum, optimistic by nature and feckless with money. She sings the wonderful song 'Marilyn Monroe' at first joyously and then with pain as she realizes her dancing days are over. Paul Crosby, wildly exuberant as a boy, is utterly believable as the man changed and broken by prison.

I should warn you that the tragic ending to the musical is something of a tear-jerker. Nothing wrong with that; it's nice to know we oldies still have feelings.

# The Three Sisters

## Orange Tree Theatre, April 2002

Since August of last year the Orange Tree Theatre, Richmond, under the directorship of Sam Walters, has been home to a repertory company, that now all but vanished and much lamented theatrical concept in which a group of actors bands together for a season and performs a repertoire of plays. Last week I went to see them enact Chekhov's *The Three Sisters*.

Anton Chekhov was born in 1860 and graduated as a doctor in 1884. He himself held that his study of medical science affected his attitude towards literature, and that he always felt he was more of a doctor than a writer. I suspect what he meant was that a knowledge of the workings of the body has much to do with an understanding of the mind.

His early plays failed, in part because his portrayal of tragedy was no longer based on a tradition of melodrama. His interest lay in the dilemma of a Russian generation wasted by the current social order, and of a people who, overwhelmed by dark and impersonal circumstances, nonetheless held on to the dream that future generations might struggle into the light. Most of Chekhov's characters extoll the ennobling benefits of work, and in this he was ahead of his time.

It's interesting to note that Harold Wilson took the opposite view and spoke volumes on the benefits of the leisure age, an utopian future in which the masses would spend their time attending arts and crafts classes and learning languages. When the great day came we all know what happened to that dream – the unemployed stayed in bed and the better off jumped up and down in numerous fitness clubs.

There's no plot to *The Three Sisters*, which is why Chekhov had a tough time making his reputation. His genius lay in dramatizing ordinary lives and ordinary consequences, something which up till then hadn't been considered the stuff of theatre. The three sisters of the title, Olga, Masha and Irma, live on an estate with their brother Andrey in a small garrison town far from Moscow, though not necessarily in miles. Moscow is the promised land: the place where life will have meaning. Andrey is part scholar, part dreamer, ultimately weak and lacking in conviction. Masha is the unfulfilled wife of the local schoolmaster. Irma, young and idealistic, has two army suitors, Baron Toozenbach and Captain Soliony, the former sweet, the latter bitter. She cares for neither – the man of her dreams is waiting in Moscow. There is another visitor, the philosophizing Battery Commander Vershinin, who falls in love with Masha, and she with him. There is a further persistent hanger-on, the military doctor, Chebutykin; now old, he is the one who constantly expresses the futility of hope.

It is Olga, apparently past all expectation of love at the age of 28, who bears the burden of the household and its numerous occupants. Powerfully portrayed by Anna Hewson, tall, immensely graceful and with a distinctive luminous voice, it is Olga who is the still, diamond centre of the play.

This is a first-rate repertory company, not a dud among them, not least Robert McBain as the doctor, David Antrobus as Andrey, Peter Wyatt as Ferapont, Jason Baughan as the school master and Helen Blatch as Anfisa. If I don't praise the others it's because in mentioning them by character I took them to be real.

At the end, Olga cries out: 'No, my dear sisters, life isn't finished for us yet . . . if we wait a little longer we shall find out why we live, why we suffer.' Alas, like me, I expect you're still waiting.

# The Syringa Tree

## Cottesloe Theatre, May 2002

*The Syringa Tree*, showing at the National's Cottesloe theatre, is set for the most part in Johannesburg during the early years of Apartheid. I went to see it on the eve of Mugabe being returned as President of Zimbabwe amid the further expulsions of white landowners. What goes around comes around!

This inspired play is performed in many voices – though predominantly that of a 6-year-old girl – by one actor, Pamela Gien, who also wrote the words. On a stage bare save for a garden swing we are persuaded to see a South African world through the eyes of a child.

Gien moves like a ballet-dancer and has an astonishing vocal range. As a writer she makes no judgements: the nannies who cared for her left their own babies in distant townships – no black child was allowed in a white area; the servants of the household were given leftovers to eat and heated their porridge on a fire in the yard. Mother spent a lot of time in bed and Daddy, a doctor, long hours at the hospital. In the programme the author writes that she didn't want to make excuses for the injustices of the time; as a little girl she accepted the way things were.

This is a clever device, for the child but dimly understands what goes on in the grown-up world around her. Daddy's gun is frightening; there are papers people have to produce if they leave the white areas; not to have the right papers is very frightening. Nanny suddenly has a black baby who can't be smuggled out of the yard and has to be hidden from the white neighbours next door. The baby hasn't got any papers either.

The play is a powerful mixture of autobiographical and fictional episodes. Grandpa, a good and kind man, is murdered by blacks. Nanny, mother of the black baby, vanishes from the household, ashamed of belonging to the same race as those who killed him. Years later, the child narrator, now grown-up and living in New York, returns home and learns that Nanny's baby was killed, aged 14, in the Soweto uprising of 1976. We are made to feel that her death is a vindication of all that has gone before; she died in a battle for freedom.

*The Syringa Tree* is a difficult piece to review: in its freshness and theatrical imagery it's unlike anything else presently in production. One can't fault either the words or the performer, except that it took time to get used to the voice of the child narrator. One feared her prattle would go on forever, yet once the other voices kicked in I could have sworn the stage was filled with actors. It is also, in my opinion, at one-and-three-quarter hours without an interval, 10 to 15 minutes too long.

In the programme the author writes: 'Carried in this story are my deepest feelings about a hauntingly beautiful place caught in unforgivable sorrow. Nobody won. And it's a story filled with joy and wishes. Some might come true.'

To that one can only add: 'How long, O Lord, how long?'

# Daisy Pulls It Off

## Lyric Theatre, June 2002

I was going to review *The Constant Wife* by Somerset Maugham, never a playwright to let one down, but then, passing the Lyric Theatre on Shaftesbury Avenue, my attention was caught by billboards featuring a group of jolly-hockey-stick girls. What a fortunate decision! *Daisy Pulls It Off*, written by Denise Deegan, directed by David Gilmore and produced by Andrew Lloyd Webber, should, if there's any justice, become a cult show, in the manner of *The Mousetrap*, though it's far superior. I thought it was a new play, and didn't realize it was first performed in Southampton nearly 20 years ago and then ran for three years in London.

On entering the auditorium one is greeted by Miss Gibson, headmistress of Grangewood School for Girls; it's 1927 and the annual school play is about to begin. The set, featuring revolving sections of a large manor house some-where on the coast, is absolutely scrumptious, and the revolving bits don't annoy. The 'gals', and there are 15 of them – wear delicious gymslips and black stockings, and thankfully there's not a trace of St Trinian's about them.

The school play is the story of Daisy Meredith, first ele-mentary school child to win a scholarship to Grangewood. She's extremely well-mannered, doesn't eat her peas with a knife and never drops her Hs. Not only does she come top in all subjects, but she proves to be ace at hockey, not a game she had the opportunity to play at her elementary school. Even worse, she becomes an immediate favourite of blue-eyed, golden-haired 'darling Clare', the head girl. Two rotten snobs in Daisy's dormitory set out to blacken her name, and she is accused of being a sneak, a thief and a cheat.

She wins through in the end, of course, and on the way manages to find the whereabouts of the secret treasure that will ensure the survival of Grangewood and the admittance of other scholarship girls, though only one at a time.

By the end, she herself has turned out to be the cousin of 'darling Clare', and the daughter of long-lost Sir David Beaumont, who lost his memory when scuttled at sea, which is a bit of a cheat really because blood will out, won't it, and it's not surprising Daisy is such a marvel.

There are two especially inspired bits of staging – one an enactment of a hockey game and the other a rescue by Daisy of the two rotters who have fallen over a cliff during a midnight feast.

This is a very good play, being gentle, clever, funny and heart-warming all at the same time, and all the gals, not just Hannah Yelland as Daisy, play their parts to perfection.

One last thing, though nothing to do with *Daisy*: when you come out of the theatre, turn right in the direction of the stage door and look up. There's a blue plaque saying that in the 18th century this part of the building housed William Hunter's School of Anatomy. It was to this very place that the body of Dr Samuel Johnson was brought for his post-mortem.

# Lady Windermere's Fan

## Haymarket Theatre, July 2002

It's not often one goes to the theatre and dwells more on the life of the playwright than on the play itself. This is what happened when I went to the Haymarket Theatre to see Peter Hall's production of *Lady Windermere's Fan*. Apart from the film, *The Picture of Dorian Gray*, and learning in adolescence the poem 'The Ballad of Reading Gaol', written when its author was imprisoned for sodomy, I was not familiar with the works of Oscar Wilde. Yet because of the poem, in particular the lines 'He does not pray with lips of clay / For his agony to pass; / Nor feel upon his shuddering cheek / The kiss of Caiaphas', I was interested in the man, and only three years ago visited the hotel in Paris in which he died and the Café Royal where he had once held court; having undergone 'refurbishment', both places proved disappointing.

The plot of *Lady Windermere's Fan* concerns the importance of keeping up an appearance of respectability, particularly when a member of the upper classes and female into the bargain. Lady W. has been married for two years to the decent Lord W., by whom she has a six-month-old son. I mention the baby because his mother doesn't give much thought to him until the second act. Another Lord is madly in love with Lady W., though I found it hard to understand why, she being such a priggish goody-goody. Suddenly Lady W. learns that her husband has been seeing the infamous Mrs Erlynne, a woman long ago cast out by society; indeed, has been giving her substantial sums of money. Worse, he wants his wife to receive her in their home. Instantly Lady W. decides she must leave, though not to a nunnery as might be expected but into the arms of the other lovesick Lord. Obviously a dark secret lies behind all this, and if Lady W. hadn't been such a prig Lord W. could have told her the truth and saved everybody a lot of trouble – but then, it would have been a shorter play.

In the second act Lady W. has to hide behind a curtain on the sudden return of her husband and his friends from their club. Quite early on the lovesick Lord says, 'We are all in the gutter, but some of us are looking at the stars,' and only a moment later comes out with the line about a cynic being 'a man who knows the price of everything and the value of nothing'. That made me think of Wilde more than ever.

Save for Googie Withers as the Duchess of Berwick, I thought the men much more comfortable in their roles than the women. Perhaps the fact that women's lives and attitudes have altered more radically than those of men was what made Joely Richardson as Lady W. and Vanessa Redgrave as Mrs Erlynne less convincing.

First produced in 1892, the play was an immediate success, presumably because members of its high-society audience, in spite of recognizing themselves, felt secure enough not to take offence. At the conclusion of the opening performance they stood and called for the author, who strolled languidly on stage holding a cigarette in one gloved hand and congratulated them on their intelligent appreciation. He added, 'I am persuaded that you think almost as highly of the play as I do.'

In the programme it says Wilde wanted the mystery of Mrs Erlynne to be revealed in the first act, but the producer of the time wouldn't agree. I think he was wrong. Wilde later, described the piece as 'one of those modern drawing-room plays with pink lampshades'. He was wrong too.

# Bombay Dreams

## Apollo Theatre, August 2002

The West End musical *Bombay Dreams* opened last week at the Victoria Apollo theatre. The score is by the Indian composer A. R. Rahman, and the book by Meera Syal, she who was responsible for the popular TV soap, *Goodness Gracious Me*. The storyline is in the Shakespearean mould and portrays corruption, murder, a lust for fame and power, and two sorts of love, one selfish, the other selfless. Needless to say, the first sort triumphs.

Akaash is a young slum dweller who dreams of becoming a Bollywood filmstar. To this end he wears tight trousers and struts about the stage singing songs at the top of his voice. Or rather he shouts them; these days the amplifier has become king. One can't dislike Akaash because he's very poor, unlikely to become a property developer and not to be blamed for wanting to better himself and secure three meals a day and a classy car. Somewhere behind that brash exterior hides a worthwhile human being, for he has a devoted friend called Sweetie who loves him. Sweetie is no ordinary bloke: he's a eunuch, and wears a frock to emphasize the fact.

The second act is better than the first, possibly because Akaash begins to show his better side and one has managed to take in and sort out the many complications of plot. There were two moments, perhaps three, when I hunched forward in my seat and forgot where I was: the first when the curtain rose (or rather, the lights came on) to show, to the accompaniment of haunting Indian music, Bombay at dawn; the next when the cast sang and danced the number 'Shakalaka Baby', but most of all when a member of the dastardly Indian Mafia put a rope about Sweetie's throat –

he was lying on the ground – placed a foot on his Adam's apple and jerked the rope upwards. This was particularly sad as he was very charming and one wished it could have been Akaash instead.

I wanted to like this show. The young cast dance and sing their socks off, and sometimes the music is catchy, if too loud. It also has a curious and rather touchingly amateurish air about it, rather like that film in which young Micky Rooney rounds up the kids in the neighbourhood and puts on an entertainment – only that, of course, was highly professional and only pretending to be otherwise.

I think what spoilt *Bombay Dreams* for me was the size of the theatre, for I sat in the back row of the stalls, and even with the binoculars provided I got the impression that the stage was a good few miles away. Also, save for the opening view of Bombay at dawn, the sets were hardly exciting and far too often a huge brown backcloth came down to hide the next scene change. I couldn't help thinking of *Sunset Boulevard*, a musical whose set was so magnificent that it wouldn't have mattered if there had been no songs at all.

There was one confusing moment at the Apollo when Akaash sang a number and suddenly a swoosh of water landed on him. I thought some pipe above had burst, but later it was explained to me that this was a joke – apparently it always rains in Bollywood films.

There are only two fates awaiting this musical. Either it comes off quite soon or it runs for years. Either way, I thought it much superior to *Cats*.

# Sleuth

## Apollo Theatre, September 2002

I've retained but a dim memory of a film called *Sleuth*, starring Laurence Olivier and Michael Caine, based on a play by Anthony Shaffer. Over time it has got mixed up with *Olivier* in a picture about a nasty Nazi dentist. Both films were awash with menace, the first underplayed, the second screaming intent.

*Sleuth*, the play, is now in revival at the Apollo Theatre, Shaftesbury Avenue, and my grandson accompanied me last week to the matinée; ten years ago, aged nine, he was referred to in this column as Darling Bertie. On his telephoning to thank me for taking him, he remarked that he had found it better than expected. This floored me, for I thought it terrific, and have since been trying to work out why he had reservations.

The plot is apparently pure Agatha Christie, albeit several notches up, a similarity that escaped me until reading various reviews in the broadsheets. Granted, there is a deep hole in the garden and splashes of blood on the stair-rods, and maybe Inspector Doppler's wig looked a bit odd, but the dialogue unravelling the mystery is surely far superior to that employed by Christie.

Peter Bowles plays Andrew, a rich and ageing husband with a fondness for electronic gadgets, whose wife is leaving him for a younger man. In Andrew's estimation the wife is vain, extravagant and selfish, yet he wants to hang on to her; it becomes obvious why in the last moments of the play.

The role of the young man, Milo, is played by Gray O'Brien, an actor I hadn't heard of and who gradually became convincing. One could argue that he lacked the cold and cheeky charm of Michael Caine, but then there is more than one way of interpreting a character. Andrew invites Milo to his home and goes to considerable lengths to make his visit unforgettable.

At this point, one wonders what the home life of the playwright was like. Shaffer, Anthony, was born in Liverpool in 1926, the elder, by five minutes, of twins. His sibling was Peter, who wrote *Amadeus*. Anthony wrote the film scripts of *Frenzy*, *The Wicker Man*, *Death on the Nile* and *Appointment With Death*. When he showed the stage script of *Sleuth* to Binkie Beaumont, it was turned down on the grounds that it wouldn't last a fortnight. In January 1970 it played that fortnight at the Theatre Royal, Brighton, received a standing ovation, was described by Laurence Olivier as 'a piece of piss' and went on to play 2,359 performances at St Martin's Theatre.

Bowles's performance in this production is excellent. There's nothing slick or debonair about him, nothing of the gent. This is a weak, sexually unsure man who is finally beaten at his own game.

To return to the vexed point of possibly why Darling Bertie didn't expect it to be any good. Plays, as written by Ibsen, Pinter, Nicols, Wesker, Shaffer, etc. – in other words, those dramatists disciplined by rules established in the past – are now becoming too involved for the young to follow. What the young demand is instant comprehension, instant gratification. I blame *Big Brother*.

# Dr Johnson and Mrs Thrale

## New Vic, October 2002

Some weeks ago I received a newspaper cutting informing me of a theatrical happening shortly to take place at the New Vic theatre in my home town of Newcastle-under-Lyme. Richard Ingrams, illustrious editor of this magazine, Raymond Banning, Professor of Piano at Trinity College and tutor of the Cambridge Piano Weekends, and *Oldie* theatre critic Beryl Bainbridge were all advertised as due to appear. I at once wrote to the magazine asking for further information and was astounded to be asked to write a critique of the forthcoming event. As a teacher of tap-dancing rather than a theatre reviewer, my pen was poised to refuse when an elderly friend sent me one of those yellow cards, so thoughtfully handed out by the Director-General of the BBC, bearing the poetic injunction, 'Cut the Crap, Make it Happen'.

On the night in question the theatre was full. Mr Ingrams as Dr Johnson and Miss Bainbridge as Mrs Thrale came on stage, bowed and sat at two round tables. Mr Banning seated himself at a very shiny black piano. The lights dimmed on the tables and concentrated on the man at the keyboard, who then proceeded to give a wonderful performance of the first movement of J. C. Bach's Sonata in G, Opus 17, No 4.

I knew nothing about Dr Johnson, who was born 293 years ago and was apparently almost as much a celebrity in his time as that footballer with the funny haircut is today. Mrs Thrale, wife of Henry, a wealthy brewer and Member of Parliament for Southwalk, became Johnson's bosom friend and confidante. He lived, on and off, in the Thrales' mansion at Streatham Park – now Common – until his death 17 years later in 1784.

The first half of the evening provided an introduction to Johnson's birth and achievements prior to his meeting with the Thrales. He was a sickly infant, failed to graduate from Oxford owing to depression, married at 22 a woman of 40 who later died of drink and opium, compiled the first proper English Dictionary, a preface to Shakespeare, several epic poems and something important entitled *The Lives of the Poets*. The second half of the entertainment consisted of readings of letters exchanged between the good Doctor and Mrs Thrale, accompanied by a moving summary of their last years together. What with Johnson's best work behind him, Henry Thrale's death from over-eating and Mrs Thrale's subsequent remarriage to her daughter's Italian singing teacher – an event which undoubtedly hastened Johnson into the grave – it was no wonder that many among us brought out our handkerchiefs. Our emotions were further played upon by Mr Banning performing pieces by Mozart and Clementi; as a tap-dancer, I am well aware that music bruises the soul.

Mr Ingrams was excellent in his part; he had authority, even though his shirt was hanging out. Mr Banning was the best dressed. Miss Bainbridge fidgeted somewhat. All the same, she quoted something I shan't forget, something Johnson wrote when his life was drawing to a close: 'I struggle hard for life. I take physick and air. My friend's chariot is always ready. We have run this morning 25 miles, and could run 48 more . . . but who can run the race with death?'

Who indeed.

# Afterplay

## Gate Theatre Dublin, November 2002

*Afterplay* by Brian Friel premiered at the Gate Theatre Dublin and is now in production at the Gielgud in Shaftesbury Avenue, It stars – and for once the description is fully justified – Penelope Wilton and John Hurt.

The action takes place in a dingy café in Moscow in the early 1920s. There is no one present except Sonya, who is sorting through a pile of letters and documents. She seems both determined to put them in order and incapable of doing so. Andrey enters, wearing evening dress and carrying a violin case. They are not quite strangers, for they met in the same café the night before and struck up some sort of conversation to do with remedies for chilblains and chapped lips. Andrey has been rehearsing all day, so he tells her, for the opening performance of *La Bohème* at the Opera House the following night. He complains that his feet are killing him after being on them for six hours. She asks if it is usual to wear evening dress for a rehearsal, and to stand upright while playing the violin. He assures her that it is.

It's obvious they are drawn to each other, but it doesn't appear to be a sexual attraction, at least not yet; rather that they share a sense of optimism, a thankfulness that life has treated them rather well. Andrey is a widower, but has two clever and prosperous children, two caring sisters and a job with the orchestra. He once had three sisters, but one, a victim of an unhappy love affair with a battery commander, shot herself. Sonya has a large country estate which in recent years has not been financially viable; after, a day at the bank ploughing through her numerous documents she has been assured it is only a matter of time before it becomes profitable again. For the rest, she has fond memories of an uncle, and an enduring and fulfilling friendship with her local doctor.

It wasn't until Sonya gave a name to her uncle and Andrey identified Masha as his dead sister that I realized *Afterplay* is the story, 20 years on, of two characters, one who appeared in Chekhov's *Uncle Vanya* and the other in *The Three Sisters*.

Of course, you could find this out if you were prepared to fork out for a programme, but it wouldn't matter if you'd never heard of Chekhov; the drama exists on its own.

There is no plot to *The Three Sisters*, or to most of his plays for that matter, which is why Chekhov had a struggle to make his reputation. Nor has *Afterplay* a plot, simply an underlying assumption, against all odds, that life will come right in the end. The odds against it coming right for Sonya and Andrey are crushing. As the evening progresses and Sonya brings a bottle of vodka out of her bag, the true version of their separate circumstances begins to emerge. When it's all out in the open they exchange addresses. He says he wants to see her again. She says that would be lovely, but she turns back at the door of the café and explains why she can't and won't. Nor must he write to her. Sadly, he agrees. When she's gone he sits down and begins to write her a letter. The spirit of Chekhov hovers above him – one must never give up hope.

This is a wonderfully real play, made even more real by the performances of Wilton and Hurt. It's as though one isn't in a theatre at all, but sitting at a shadowy table in the same café, dining alone and overhearing every word.